girls' ministry 101

Ideas for Retreats, Small Groups, and Everyday Life with Teenage Girls

Whitney Prosperi

GRAND RAPIDS, MICHIGAN 49530

ZONDERVAN.COM/
AUTHORTRACKER

Youth Specialties

Girls' Ministry 101: Ideas for Retreats, Small Groups, and Everyday Life with Teenage Girls
Copyright © 2006 by Whitney Prosperi

Youth Specialties products, 300 South Pierce Street, El Cajon, CA 92020 are published by Zondervan, 5300 Patterson Avenue Southeast, Grand Rapids, MI 49530.

Library of Congress Cataloging-in-Publication Data

Prosperi, Whitney.
  Girls ministry 101 : ideas for retreats, small groups, and everyday life with teenage girls / Whitney Prosperi.
    p. cm.
  ISBN-10: 0-310-26747-1 (pbk.)
  ISBN-13: 978-0-310-26747-1 (pbk.)
  1. Church work with teenagers. 2. Teenage girls--Religious life. I. Title.

  BV4447.P755 2006
  259'.23--dc22

2006001023

Creative Team: Dave Urbanski, Erika Hueneke, Laura Gross, Doug Davidson, and Mark Novelli
Cover Design by Holly Sharp
Printed in the United States

---

07 08 09 10 • 10 9 8 7 6 5 4 3

Dedication

For my mom and dad—I love you.

Acknowledgments

Behind every book are some great people who make it happen. I want to thank the staff at Youth Specialties for its support and encouragement and all the friends and family who faithfully prayed for me during the process. Thank you also to my husband, Randy, for always cheering me on. You're wonderful, and I love you very much.

I want to say a special thank you to the following people for sharing their ideas, experiences, and dreams with me. Without each of you, this book would have never been written. You are my heroes as you serve the girls God has put in your lives and ministries. May he continue to work powerfully in and through you.

Janée Angel	Shaun Hawkins	Julie Romero
Angie Black	Becky Henderson	Shauna Rushing
Amanda Bostwick	Amy Jacober	Joy Ryan
Kelly Callison	Dyanna Jones	Michelle Sanders
Kelly Carter	Lucy Koy	Christi Schreckengost
Meghan Charles	Jessi Lawson	Leann Spruell
Beth Anne Dane	Cheryl Miller	Donna Stuart
Margaret Denman	Sarah Miller	Gina Taylor
Chrissie Dunham	Beverly Parrish	Maria Turner
Michelle Gray	Alissa Peeler	Bethany Walsh
Sarah Harmeyer	Heather Rogero	Emily Walsh

Contents

Doing Something About It

Did you know that one of the fastest growing staff positions in churches today is a girls' minister? It's true. More and more, members of church staffs and church boards are beginning to recognize the unique needs of teenage girls—and they're doing something about it.

If you're reading this book, then either you're already involved with, or you're interested in becoming involved with, a ministry to teenage girls. You may be a youth minister who realizes that over half of your youth group is made up of these unusual creatures called females. Maybe you're looking for some new ideas for meeting the needs of the girls in your ministry.

Or maybe you're a woman who volunteers in an existing ministry, or you're a mom of a daughter in a youth group. You picked up this book to confirm that you're not alone. You want to know that there are others who share your passion to reach out to teen girls. Be encouraged! God is raising up women—young and old—to be examples and mentors to the girls of this generation.

Regardless of where you're coming from, consider this book an idea generator. In the following pages you'll find lots of helpful ideas to use with the girls in your specific situation, whether it's a church or parachurch ministry, small church or megachurch. The ideas come from girls' ministers who've used them. You can try what you think will work for you and adapt any idea to fit your ministry. This book will not only give you helpful tips from these veteran women, but it will also spark your own creativity.

chapter one

The Who, What, and Why of Girls' Ministry

Why Have a Girls' Ministry?

Today's teenage girls deal with complex and pressing issues that their parents wouldn't have dreamed of when they were growing up. Their temptations are serious and, in some cases, life threatening. Their friends are most likely sexually active, and the girls you work with may be as well. They deal with constant pressure to perform, achieve, and be picture-perfect and ultra-thin. Girls are dealing with eating disorders in record numbers. They are often the targets of sexual abuse or harassment. Many struggle with depression, cutting, and substance abuse. If they want drugs, they can get them easily. In short, while girls in the United States have more rights, freedoms, and opportunities than ever before, they also have a growing number of problems that are deeply rooted in being female.

Girls are pressed on every side. Many are forced to deal with adult issues even though they lack the maturity and knowledge to handle them. And while girls who come to church and are involved in youth group have a better chance of escaping many of these pitfalls than some of their unchurched friends, they will still face undeniable temptations and problems.

Girls' ministry is crucial. Many churches have adults designated as youth ministers, but even when those people happen to be women, it's ideal if churches appoint females to whom the girls can go exclusively. I know from personal experience that if you stand in front of a youth group and tell them a woman is available for the girls to talk with, that woman had better be prepared to listen! I listened—to every imaginable issue, it seemed. Many girls just need to be heard and validated.

Girls crave someone who can relate to them and understand their unique struggles. They desperately need women outside their families and circles of friends who will be objective and give them godly advice.

For the male youth workers reading this book: I'm not saying you *can't* minister to girls—obviously you can! You do it every day. But youth workers, male and female alike, can share only so much with students of the opposite gender. There are limits and boundaries.

So if you have women on your staff who can do this, whether paid or volunteer, that's great news! If you don't yet have women on your staff, start praying for and recruiting female volunteers so the girls in your group can have a minister to turn to when they really need her.

These are just a few reasons why churches should consider equipping women—whether paid staffers or volunteers—to lead and minister to girls. It's not because we need to create male-only and female-only youth groups, but we need to offer conversational outlets and sources of care and comfort for girls whenever they need them.

Who Should Minister to Girls?

Large churches may have the resources to hire women who can work full-time on the youth staff and be responsible for the girls; other churches may hire part-time female youth ministers. Many churches don't have such resources—but they can still find female volunteers to lead the girls.

Whatever the case, it's important to make sure the girls' minister isn't fresh out of high school. Determining maturity is crucial here. Girls will look to her as a mentor, leader, teacher, and advice-giver. Much prayer should be directed toward deciding who should lead this vital aspect of the student ministry. In most cases, the girls' ministry (and girls' minister) will fall under the leadership and vision of the overall youth ministry. For this reason, it's important that whoever is chosen to lead the girls' ministry is also willing to work in harmony with the leadership of the senior pastor and the youth minister.

When I started as the girls' minister at a church that had never had one before, my boss and the other staff did everything they possibly could to, as they called it, "elevate the position." They wanted to make sure the students knew I'd be working alongside the other youth staff and would be equally as involved in planning and leading. I remember being thankful for their leadership and foresight, as it made my transition easier.

One note: Maybe you have a heart for girls' ministry but feel that you have no platform. You believe you're called to girls' ministry, but it seems no one is willing to give you a chance. I'm often asked the question, "How do I get started so I can minister to girls on a church staff or in another 'official role'?" If you're asking this question, the following encouragement is just for you.

Remember that God is the one who validates your calling. A position or title behind your name doesn't make you better at ministering to girls. The work of God in you and through you is the only thing that can make a lasting impact. Allow God to use you where you are. If there are girls living in your neighborhood or apartment complex, reach out to them. If there are young women at your work or in your family, minister to them. Let

God use you right now—right where you are. He has placed you there for this season and his purpose so he can use you (Acts 17:26-27). Will you let him work through you now, instead of waiting for him to give you a bigger platform later? Trust him and take one day at a time. You don't have to push doors open in Jesus' name. Serve where you are and know that he is perfectly capable of expanding your influence in his timing.

> "Lead by example. Not by words, but by actions."
>
> —CHERYL MILLER, CHAMPION FOREST BAPTIST CHURCH

What Are the Benefits of Having a Girls' Minister?

If you were to ask this question of youth ministers who are already leading healthy girls' ministries in their churches, they would undoubtedly list the following benefits:

- **Girls have someone to talk to.** As any man knows, females speak the same language. We relate to one another. We understand the delicate emotional seasons of a female's life. Teenage girls are dealing with so many sensitive issues. Given the choice, most girls would feel more comfortable talking with a female youth worker instead of a male. (The male would feel more comfortable as well.) A girls' minister can offer girls genuine love and encouragement that many of them don't get at home or from their friends.

- **A girls' minister offers a female perspective in planning youth events.** When a youth staff plans events and brainstorms ideas, a girls' minister offers a fresh and different perspective. She can help think of activities that would

appeal to females as well as males. Having a girls' minister can mean having a more balanced student ministry.

- **Having a girls' minister provides protection for male leadership.** Whenever the male youth minister counsels a girl, the girls' minister can sit in the room with them. After events or meetings, the girls' minister can also wait to leave until all of the females are gone. This protects the males in leadership from ever being in situations where they are alone with young women. She can also be a trustworthy liaison when gender issues arise within the youth ministry.

- **A girls' minister can plan girl-only events.** It's amazing how girls let their guards down when no guys are around. It's so refreshing for them to be together, enjoying themselves and one another without the pressure of how they look or who is watching them. A girls' minister can plan events that range from a simple sleepover to an elaborate retreat or night on the town. Girls love these times with their girlfriends, enjoying something planned especially for them.

- **Discipleship—a girls' minister can lead all-girl Bible studies and small groups.** While Bible study with the whole youth group is beneficial, girls in a smaller group can be transparent in ways they wouldn't be in mixed company. A girls' minister can lead the girls and train other leaders to teach as well. She is in touch with girls' needs and can offer curriculum especially geared for them.

- **A girls' minister is a role model to the girls.** Our culture offers some pretty poor role models for young women. A girls' minister is someone whom girls can look to and pattern their lives after. They can follow her as she follows Christ. She can help girls as they seek after God and the calling and purpose he has for each of their lives and as they learn about developing their spiritual gifts and life skills.

I have heard so many youth ministers say they didn't realize they needed girls' ministries until their churches started them. When they designated women as their girls' ministers, and these women began planning events, the girls responded, brought their friends, and took more ownership in the ministries. The girls even began to assume leadership roles, and many of them took their first steps in the ministries God had especially for them.

In the following chapters, we'll look at some starting places for the "hows" of girls' ministry, and we'll also discuss other practical ideas from girls' ministers all over the country. Some of them serve in small churches, some in large, but they all have one thing in common—they are called to minister to the girls of this generation. As you read, ask God what he wants to do in your ministry. It may be something that resembles an idea you read about here, or it could be completely different. He is an infinitely creative God who knows exactly how to meet the girls in your ministry right where they are.

chapter two

Practical Advice for Starting Out

Building Relationships

If you're starting in a brand-new position as girls' minister at your church, you probably have a mixed bag of emotions and thoughts. Maybe you're overwhelmed by all of the girls' needs and problems. You probably want to get to know each and every girl and all of the adult volunteers. There is so much to do—and you want to start it all *right now*.

Maybe you're the youth minister who has just appointed a girls' minister at your church. You've waited and prayed for someone to fill this position, and now she's finally here. You couldn't be happier—and you couldn't have more work to give her. Where do you start?

While the temptation for most of us is to just jump in and do something—anything—that's usually not the best starting place. For the first six months or so on the job, I suggest that girls' ministers focus mainly on building relationships. Time spent talking with and, more importantly, listening to girls can give you a perspective and wisdom that will make a difference in all that you do for years to come.

If you're new to the church, take some time to find out who the student leaders are and get to know them—but don't stop there. Find out who the *potential* leaders are, too. There may be several girls who seem as quiet as they come but have the gift of leadership within them. Organize events where the focus is on talking.

A friend of mine who started as the girls' minister at a large church organized a sleepover for each grade in the youth group. During the wee hours of the morning, she got to know the core group of girls. She also talked with the quiet girls who wouldn't necessarily open up in a large group. Now she looks back on those early sleepovers as the place where a lot of her existing relationships with girls began. And the more she got to know the personality of the group, the more she understood what types of events they would respond to. She made it a point to learn about her girls' interests and also paid attention to where they were in their spiritual walks. She listened to their concerns and problems. After she felt she had a good "pulse" of the group, she started prayerfully planning for the next year.

> "Pursue relationships with girls. Don't wait for them to come to you."
>
> —ALISSA PEELER, SECOND BAPTIST CHURCH

While events are wonderful tools for getting students excited and bringing them together, most ministry takes place in one-on-one relationships. That's why it's important that you make spending time with girls a top priority. They may or may not remember some awesome program you planned, but they will most certainly recall the way you listened to their problems and carved out time to be with them on their good and bad days.

> "If we want our girls to know Christ and make him known, we must think strategically and take advantage of every minute we're with them. Our roles are spiritual mentors, not buddies."
>
> —MARGARET DENMAN

The Youth Staff

Along with getting to know the girls in your youth ministry, it's essential to build relationships with the other staff. If it's possible to go away on a staff retreat, take advantage of that opportunity. The more uni-

fied the staff is, the better prepared you'll be to come together to meet common goals.

Be proactive in building relationships with youth workers as well. Many of these servants were probably around for a while before you came along, so they know the students much better than you do. Becoming allies with these teachers and volunteers will make a huge difference in the effectiveness of your ministry. Figure out how you can get to know them and then combine efforts.

Relating to Male Staffers (A Caution)

One word of advice: If you are the only woman working with a youth staff full of men, it's wise and vital to set appropriate boundaries. While you may know your motives are pure and innocent, you never want to cause someone else to question them. Guard yourself against being alone with another male on the youth staff. If you set wise boundaries, you won't have to worry about rumors, gossip, or misunderstandings.

When I was hired to join a formerly all-male youth staff, I prayed that God would help me set appropriate boundaries. I felt I shouldn't ride in a car alone with any one of the guys I worked with. While our relationships were pure, like brother-sister, I knew that not everyone in our community would know that. There was no reason to cause anyone to wonder if something questionable was going on. Most of the time several of us rode together in a car when we were going somewhere—but when there were only two of us, we took separate cars. Maybe that's not the most economic or environmentally friendly way to travel, but it kept us safe from questions and rumors.

Make it a point to pray about what boundaries God wants you to use. It only takes one rumor to cast doubt on someone, and the results can be disastrous. As Matthew 10:16 says, "Be as shrewd as snakes and as innocent as doves."

Parents

Make sure your girls' parents know that you're available to them as well. Encourage them to come to events and see what's going on. Every now and then, plan something for the girls that will also involve their moms, dads, or both. You could ask the dads to serve the girls during a banquet or ask the moms to decorate for an event. It's also a good idea to periodically offer a seminar for parents so they can hear about some of the issues their teens are dealing with. When you know the different family situations, you'll be better able to minister to the girls' needs.

Also, as you build relationships with parents, you'll probably develop a wonderful support system to help you. Some of these parents may turn out to be your most active volunteers. Remember that girls' ministry is a family ministry, so be sure to keep the lines of communication open with the parents.

"Build relationships with your girls' parents. Support them and let them know you're on their team. The more you know girls' parents, the more insight you'll have into your girls' lives."

—MARGARET DENMAN

Female Volunteers

You may want to schedule time with some of the key female youth volunteers. Ask them what they see as the strengths of the youth ministry. Invite them to tell you where they think it needs to grow. Spend time listening to them—and not as much time talking about what *you* want to do. Serve them as they are

serving students. In many ways, they will have more inroads to the hearts of students than you will, at least at first. Find out the strengths of these servant leaders and empower them to do the work of the ministry. And finally, pray with them and for them. Many of them may be tired of giving without seeing any change in students. As Galatians 6:9 says, encourage them to "not become weary in doing good."

Narrowing Your Scope

In the course of writing this book, I attended a gathering of several girls' ministers. When I asked them to share practical advice for someone just starting out, I heard several common themes come up again and again. One that was consistently repeated was focus. As you start in a new role, it's important to designate what is within your realm of responsibilities—and what isn't.

Job Description

First of all, make sure you have a job description. You may receive one from your boss or the church, or you may have the privilege of working with the student ministry team to create your own. Whatever the case, a job description will provide you with a filter through which you can run things. It will help you determine how to spend your time and energy, and it will also provide you with a tool to assess how you're doing in the role God has given you. When you have a job description that you and your coworkers have agreed on, not only will you be better able to do the job you were hired to do, but you'll also be more productive while you're doing it.

Since girls' ministry typically falls under the leadership of the student ministry, much of what the girls' minister does will be general youth ministry. For instance, as a girls' minister, I was responsible (along with the rest of the youth staff) for recruiting youth workers, planning events, and ordering curriculum. In terms of the focus of the student ministry and the events workload, the usual philosophy was "All hands on deck." That meant that when it came time to plan a discipleship weekend, we all shared the responsibility.

In addition to general youth ministry, my job description included planning all-girl events, discipling girls, and meeting one-on-one with them for the purpose of mentoring and spiritual formation.

Expectations

If girls' minister is a new role at your church, it's especially important that you sit down with your boss and discuss expectations and responsibilities. Determine how you'll be measured in terms of an employee review, what your days off will be, and the hours you're expected to work. While emergencies or special situations will make it necessary to adjust those hours at times, for the most part, you should plan to work the hours that you and your boss establish.

You'll also want to determine boundaries with your staff. Maybe you'll decide that you don't want to receive calls on your day off, unless it's an absolute emergency. Or you may ask your staff to protect your cell phone number, by giving it to students only in special circumstances. Whatever boundaries you prayerfully set, make sure you live by them and encourage those you work with to respect them as well.

It's important that the other members of the staff and the youth volunteers understand your job description. That way they won't ask you to do things you weren't hired to do. One girls' minister I spoke with recalled how it is easy to fall into "secretary syndrome," where people ask you to do things that aren't in your job description, either because a secretary is backed up or because you're efficient at doing that kind of work. Sometimes it's easy to take on responsibilities that aren't ours because we feel guilty or we can easily do them ourselves. But it's important that you learn to draw boundary lines between the tasks that are most beneficial for you and those that aren't. Of course there are exceptions to this rule when things are especially hectic or there is a need to serve, so pray for wisdom regarding what to take on and what to defer to another.

Vision Casting

If you are the "pioneer" of girls' ministry at your church, remember to be patient as others buy into the vision. It may take some time for the other staff and the parents to understand and trust that what you are doing is valid. But as they see you meeting a need, they will offer support and encouragement. The great thing is that you are casting the vision and can take the ministry in whatever direction you feel God leading you.

Share your ideas with anyone who will listen. It will keep you accountable to what God has put on your heart. Secondly, pass the vision along to others and inspire them to join you. Above all, remember to have patience with yourself and others as you allow God to use you in the changing face of youth ministry.

Goal Setting

You may also want to set goals with your coworkers. You might evaluate the number of girls you meet with each week or the types of events you plan. You'll obviously want to determine these objectives after some significant time in prayer. Setting goals and sharing them with other staff and volunteers will hold you accountable and allow you to measure how well you are accomplishing what you feel God has led you to do.

Establishing a Support System

Ask God to send you a few women who will pray for you daily and keep what you share with them confidential. You may want to meet weekly with a woman or a small group for prayer and encouragement. In those meetings, make it a priority to hold each other accountable regarding your private time with God. Let these people ask you the personal, hard questions, and then be honest with them about where you struggle.

Seek out the wise counsel of older women who can see what you can't see in your life. These women will be invaluable mentors to you as you invest in your girls. When you need it, don't

"When you go guns-a-blazing by yourself, you'll get stripped of your weapons. God never wants us to go it alone. Make sure you're accountable to more than one person. You may want to ask friends or some older women to partner with you in this way. Have them ask you the hard personal questions about areas where you struggle. Make sure they know how you are really doing"

—CHERYL MILLER, CHAMPION FOREST BAPTIST CHURCH

hesitate to ask for help in whatever form necessary. The more support you have, the more effective you will be at ministering to girls. Lone rangers burn out fast. Everyone needs support and prayer—especially those in ministry. Make sure you establish this habit early.

Teaming Up

You may also want to find and plan to meet regularly with women from other congregations in your community who have a passion for girls' ministry. It's a good idea to plan a monthly lunch at a central location for the purpose of networking, sharing ideas, and praying together. This will enable you to find encouragement in the ministry God has given you, while at the same time you'll battle the tendency to focus inward on your own church, girls, and ministry responsibilities. Knowing what is going on in the broader body of Christ will give you a bigger perspective on what God is doing in your community.

You may even want to physically share in each other's ministries. You and another girls' minister could exchange speaking time at each other's girls' events—you speak at her event and then she speaks at yours. This way the girls get to hear from a fresh voice, and you can bring godly women before them without exhausting your budget on honorariums and travel.

"Meet with other girls' ministers to share ideas, encourage one another, laugh, and play together. Every now and then you may want to get together for a special event. Make sure that you know other girls' ministers who are not in your denomination."

—CHERYL MILLER, CHAMPION FOREST BAPTIST CHURCH

Every now and then you may want to partner with other girls' ministers for a common event. Pooling resources will allow you to invite someone to speak or lead worship that you wouldn't be able to bring in on your own. It will also bring girls together from the surrounding area and allow them to experience worship with others from different backgrounds or church denominations.

"I meet with a group of women from other churches about once a month. We discuss the issues we're dealing with in our own ministries and encourage one another with prayer. We also plan an activity for each meeting. For example, our first get-together was at a paint-your-own-pottery shop. For our second meeting we all brought four songs that described where we were spiritually and in our ministries. We take turns setting the agenda, and we all greatly benefit from these meetings."

—LUCY KOY, ST. MARTIN'S EPISCOPAL CHURCH

Charting Your Course

Ideas Journal

As you start this new ministry, you'll be tempted to try every idea you've ever had. Maybe you're a visionary and creative thoughts just pop into your head as you're driving down the street or taking a shower. As soon as you begin planning for one event, you're bombarded with great new ideas for 10 other projects. If this describes you, thank God for the creativity he has placed within you. Consider keeping a journal of ideas so when you think of something new, you can just grab a pen and begin brainstorming. Keep these ideas and occasionally pray over them, asking God to give you wisdom as to which one, if any, he wants you to pursue next. When you receive confirmation to go forward with something, get it on your calendar as soon as possible. That way the "tyranny of the urgent" won't rob you of what you feel God has led you to do.

Many ministries seem to go from one event to the next, with no real direction or course. So before you start to fill your calendar with a bunch of good ideas, ask God to give you a funnel for deciding which things you should and shouldn't do. You might write down a list of criteria for regular and special events you will plan. For example, if you feel that a lot of non-Christian girls are involved in your ministry, you may want to make sure the gospel is shared at most every event. That might be your top priority for the next season of your ministry. If discipleship is the focus of the next year, you might place an emphasis on teaching and memorizing Scripture. Before you begin planning an event, make sure it fulfills the purpose you feel God has given to you.

Ask Your Girls for Ideas

It's also wise to have a small group of girls and women whom you respect who'll be available to serve as your sounding boards. Before you make any drastic changes in the ministry, seek their insights. They might see some details or concerns that you've missed in your excitement over a new idea. They will also be able to provide encouragement and confirmation as you try something new.

Pray

Before you jump into your role and responsibilities, spend a lot of time in prayer, asking God what he wants to do. Ask for his direction and remember that this is "girls' ministry"—not *your* ministry. To be exact, it is God's ministry. Ask him to guide you in decisions, give you wisdom, and keep you seeking him first.

When you're starting out and as you go forward, keep prayer a priority. Establish the discipline of praying for your girls early on. If it's a habit, it will be easier to protect it when things get busy. If you do everything for your girls—from offering them great advice to planning incredible events—but you don't pray for them, you will have failed. In the secret work of prayer, you release them into God's powerful hands. Don't make the mistake of neglecting to pray diligently for your girls.

You may want to determine a name or a symbol for the girls' ministry. A friend of mine chose the daisy because, to her, it represented the blooming of the girls in her ministry. Daisies remind her that God takes care of the needs of delicate flowers and that he will all the more care for his precious girls. You could encourage girls to decide on the symbol as a group or have a contest where they come up with a symbol and explain why your group should choose it. Or you could prayerfully choose one on your own and then let them know what it is in a creative way. For Cheryl's girls, the daisy will always remind them of God's extraordinary love for them. Pick something that will hold meaning for them each time they see it. Some of your girls will carry the significance of that symbol with them for the rest of their lives.

Margaret shared with me a powerful story about praying for her girls. She writes each one's name on a notecard and keeps the spiral-bound cards next to her bed. Then she prays through the names in the morning or as she's about to go to sleep. Margaret figures she probably prays for every girl once a month. A few years ago she became discouraged because she hadn't seen many of the girls in a while. She'd been considering removing some names from the spiral when she happened to sit next to a girl at church one Sunday morning. This girl began asking Margaret questions about Christianity and decided she was going to start attending church regularly. Margaret recognized this young woman's name from her prayer cards. Just when Margaret was about to stop praying for her, the

girl showed up. Margaret realized that not only had God been working in this girl's life, but he'd also been answering Margaret's prayers. This was her confirmation to keep praying.

Whatever system you choose, make sure you keep the discipline of prayer a priority. It's the most important thing you can do for your girls.

Going Forward with Confidence

Inadequacy—it's perhaps one of the most paralyzing feelings we encounter. If you've never struggled with it, skip to the next section. But if you're like most of us, then these words may be just for you. It's so easy to face a new ministry, or even a familiar one, with the fear that you won't make a difference. Maybe you're afraid you won't say or do the right thing. You're worried you'll just mess up.

But we're all going to miss opportunities or say the wrong things at one point or another. We aren't perfect, and we certainly have the potential, in our own strength, to get others and ourselves into trouble.

The good news is that ministry isn't all up to us. We are just instruments. God is the one who changes lives. So take some pressure off of yourself.

If you struggle with feelings of inadequacy, you may want to ask someone to partner in prayer with you about it. Memorize some verses that remind you that God is your sufficiency. He's the one who brings the results. Allow him to change you from someone who depends on yourself to someone who relies on him fully.

When You Mess Up...

If you do mess up (and you will), make the situation right, set your eyes on Christ, and move on. Resist the tendency to go over past mistakes again and again. We can all think of things we wish we'd done differently and changes we could have made. We must trust that God can work in spite of us.

Will the Students Like Me?

Don't let the fear that students won't like you hold you back. Your calling is to love, serve, and speak truth to them. If you're constantly worried that you'll offend if you talk straight with them, then students may never hear what they need to hear. Say what God has called you to say. When you feel you must confront a girl about an issue, pray about it; but when you feel the time is right, speak the truth in love. Be specific with her if you're confronting her about her language, lifestyle, or some other concern. Keeping silent means you're condoning the destructive choices a girl may be making. If you don't share the truth with her, she may never hear the words that will set her free.

The more grounded you are in Christ, the more "usable" you'll be in his hands. You'll find a freedom that comes with knowing who you are and what he has called you to be. You'll resist the temptation to let ministry define you. Instead, you'll let his Word define who you are and how you minister to girls.

Belonging to God first

Nothing is more fulfilling than allowing God to use us to touch others' lives. And at the same time, nothing is more draining. That's why it's crucial that as you minister to girls, you constantly stay connected to God. You've probably heard that you can't give what you haven't received. If you're always giving, always with girls, and always involved in "spiritual events," you will burn out—fast!

Determine right now that your first priority will be your relationship with God. Do you place your time with God above everything else in your life—your comfort? Your things? Your recreation? Relationships? Ministry? Even the girls you minister to? If God is first, the rest will fall into place. If he's not, the rest will fall apart. God created you for himself. He created you to worship and know him first—not to minister. Ministry comes as the overflow. It isn't our primary purpose. The reason we have breath today is to know him.

The more girls' ministers I've talked with, the more I've heard them say this again and again in different ways: Don't neglect your relationship with God so you can "do more ministry." We're all tempted to do it. I was, and many of the women I've talked with shared the same struggle. There are so many girls with so many needs, but there's so little time. It's very easy to "cheat" God. We sleep a little later and tell ourselves we'll pray on the way to work. We let our study for a lesson become our quiet time. While it's good to teach out of the overflow of what we're learning, studying to teach shouldn't be the only time we spend in the

·

Bible. We need to prioritize learning, memorizing, and meditating on his Word for ourselves.

It's tempting to be around the things of God and miss him. When that happens, we lose the mystery and pleasure in our relationship with God. We don't embrace the joy of drawing close to him, and we treat the spiritual markers in our students' lives with casualness and irreverence. We can slip into giving God our leftover time, which also results in students receiving our "spiritual leftovers." More than that, we put ourselves in a vulnerable position for compromise and temptation.

"It's a challenge to take time with God. It's hard to be still. Sometimes you'll almost feel guilty unplugging from work to spend time with God, but you must do it."

—JULIE ROMERO, FIRST BAPTIST CHURCH

Make sure you're in a Bible study with others your age and that you spend time with people who spiritually invest in you. It's tempting to let our lives become all about the ministry, but that's the first step to an out-of-balance life. Make sure you take time to nurture your spiritual, social, and physical needs regularly. You are a child of God first, and a minister after that.

What about you? Do you neglect your spiritual walk when things get busy? When you're giving the most is when you need to receive the most. The more time you spend with students—giving to them, talking with them, and teaching them—the more time you need to spend at Jesus' feet listening to him and getting to know him more intimately. Will you prioritize time for yourself to be with him each day? Will you protect it at all costs?

"I used to rack my brain trying to be creative and to make every time together an event. I finally wised up. My girls didn't care about being entertained or wowed. What they wanted was time with me. I've finally stopped doing more than I can do. When I'm able, I still try to plan something special. However, most weeks it's soup and crackers and time with these young women and God."

—AMY JACOBER, AZUSA PACIFIC UNIVERSITY

You may want to schedule a personal retreat every so often, where you and God spend an extended time together. Maybe there's someone at your church who will let you borrow their lake house, or maybe you can just visit a park for the day with your Bible and journal. You may want to schedule one day a week when you spend extra time with God, praying over different aspects of your life and ministry. It's wise to plan these refueling times—and then keep the dates. They are great for rest, refocusing, and self-examination. In those minutes and hours alone with God, you'll hear his voice and be changed. These times will make all the difference between experiencing a productive and fruitful ministry and suffering from burnout.

The most important thing you can do for those you disciple is to walk with God. Girls will notice that God's presence is near and around you. They will remember that God used you—sometimes in spite of you. Make your purpose to know God, and the girls you minister to will be challenged to do the same.

"Don't let preparation for Bible study be your quiet time. When you're studying to teach, you have a totally different mindset. Make sure you carve out time for personal Bible study."

—MARGARET DENMAN

chapter three

Building Relationships

"One thing that I've been learning in ministering to girls is that discipleship and ministry isn't investing just that one hour a week that often begins to seem more like a task—it means simply living life together. Little things make a huge difference—like taking a girl grocery shopping with you or teaching her how to cook, running errands together or hanging out in coffee shops. Simply showing you care and being willing to involve her in your life is huge."

—MICHELLE GRAY, SECOND BAPTIST CHURCH

Twenty years from now, the girls in your ministry won't recall the great events you planned, and most of the words you've spoken to them will be a distant memory—but they will always treasure the relationships they built with you. They will remember sitting up late, talking and laughing at a retreat. They'll treasure the fact that you took time to come to their sporting events or school plays. The time you invest in girls now will affect them for the rest of their lives. In this chapter we'll look at some ways to build relationships with the girls in your ministry.

For some this may come naturally. You might be the type of person who connects with the people in line with you at the post office. For others who may be more task-driven, you may need reminders to place people over plans. Of course, as in all things, we must find the balance. If we're always with students, we won't have time for planning, follow-up, and the administrative tasks that must be done. That's why we must continually ask God to give us wisdom in investing our time.

The Difference

Meaningful relationships—students are hungry for them. You've probably already realized that when you give a girl your undivided attention, she soaks it up. Sadly most teenagers don't get that kind of attention very often. In many cases, their parents are pulled in numerous directions. And while today's students connect with each other more often than any past generation (thanks to cell phones and e-mail), they crave quality "real time" with others.

A friend of mine says she takes every opportunity to speak truth to her girls. She says that even though we may feel like we've said it so often that they're immune to our words, our girls still need to hear that they are cherished and valuable to God. She believes that all girls, whether they know it or not, desire to be beautiful and loved in someone's eyes. We can point them to the One who can fill those needs. Don't hesitate to verbalize life to them whenever you get the chance. Carving out time with them is the first step in this process.

Where to Start

The Name Game

It may seem mundane, but remembering your girls' names is the first challenge. While some people recall names more easily, most of us have to work at it. Remembering students' names is just like any other skill—most of the time it takes practice. Maybe you could impose a self-prescribed crash-course on remembering their names. Plenty of resources are available to help you, and just improving this simple skill will enable you to better connect with your students.

Michelle told me about a creative way to learn girls' names. The ministry she worked with took digital pictures of each

student and then burned the pictures to CDs for every minister and volunteer. She says it helped everyone to learn names, and then they were able to interact more personally with the students. Because more adults remembered the students' names, it made a huge difference in how connected the girls felt.

Getting More Elaborate

Alissa, a girls' minister at a large church, told me that when she started her job, the number of girls in her ministry overwhelmed her. She quickly decided to invent a tool to help her learn girls' names. She typed up a "bio sheet" for the girls to fill out and return to her. On this sheet were several questions to answer and a place to attach a picture. She said these sheets gave her an advantage in learning the girls' names.

Meghan, another girls' minister, uses a sheet called "What's Your Story?" If you use something like this, you might want to ask the girls to write what encourages them. Or include a place for them to write their lunch period, followed by the question, "Would it be fun for you if I came to hang out with you during lunch, or is that a time when you usually catch up with friends?" If you decide to ask your girls to fill out sheets like this, be as creative as you wish. Ask whatever you want to know about them.

Alissa organizes the girls' completed sheets by their year in school and then puts each grade level in its own binder. She'll flip through the binders periodically to brush up on the girls' names, and then call some of the girls—just to visit. Some-

"When we went into the ministry, we started with the file system first. What a blessing it is 10 years later—resources at your fingertips!"

—DYANNA JONES, HENDERSON HILLS BAPTIST CHURCH

times when she calls a girl, Alissa asks her to bring three of her friends to hang out after school the next day.

The following is a sample of her Girls' Ministry Questionnaire that you can reproduce and use with the girls in your ministry.

Girls' Ministry Questionnaire

Name_____ Grade_____

Address_____

_____

_____

City_____ State_____ Zip_____

Phone_____ Birthday_____

School_____

E-Mail_____

List the names of some friends whom you love to hang out with:

_____

_____

Please attach your picture here.

Getting to Know YOU...

What are you involved in at school?

What is your favorite movie and why?

What is your favorite CD right now?

What is your favorite restaurant? Favorite flavor of ice cream? Favorite soda?

If you had $1,000 to spend, where would you go and what would you buy?

Choose one of the following (don't worry—it's just between you and me!)

☐ I don't have a relationship with God.

☐ I am moving away from God.

☐ I am stuck in the middle in my relationship with God— I'm not moving toward him or away from him.

☐ I am growing slowly in my relationship with God.

☐ I am passionate about my relationship with God.

Make Contact

Get Tech Savvy!

The girls in your youth group are probably very accessible. Most of them have cell phones, and they probably spend more time on the Internet than you spend sleeping. Take advantage of these ways to connect with your students. Communication is key.

My friend Angie says, "Text and instant messaging is God's greatest gift to student ministry." While she's waiting in lines or sitting in traffic, she spends the time sending messages to her girls. When a student comes to mind, she usually makes it a point to make contact with her. Because of this, Angie is usually one of the first to know what's going on in her girls' lives.

Janée keeps in touch with many of her girls by e-mail. She often types out her prayers for their lives and e-mails them to the girls. Some have told her that when they read her prayers, they feel like she's in the same room praying for them. It's a valuable way to connect spiritually with girls, and they will have these prayers to look back at from time to time.

You might want to program some of your girls' phone numbers into your cell phone. For instance, if you have a small group of girls who meet for Bible study, add their numbers to your phone. You won't ever have to go searching for their numbers when it's time to communicate with them, and you can easily call one of them if she misses a week. Margaret shared that her Bible study group's name was CRAZE. When she plugged the members' numbers into her cell phone, she typed "CRAZE Cindy" or "CRAZE Sue." Then on the way home from Bible study, she'd call any girls who were absent that day. She knew that if she put it off, she might forget. The call doesn't take a lot of time, and it lets girls know they are valued and missed when they aren't there.

Birthdays

Remember them. Since there's a space for the girls' birthdays on their bio sheets, you could set up a system where you call or send them an e-mail on that day. You might want to send them a card with an herbal teabag in it. Or if you have a little extra money in the budget, you could send them a gift card for a cup of java at the local coffee shop. Be as creative as you want. Maybe you and some of the girl's friends could "kidnap" her and take her out for a small celebration. For you to remember her birthday and make contact on her special day will show her that she's important to you.

Time

Carving out time for all of our responsibilities is perhaps one of the biggest challenges of girls' ministry. We utilize our time best when we invest in someone else's life. That's why it's crucial that we prioritize time best with our girls. Weekly events are great for getting to know girls and giving them a platform to open up to us. Whether you make it a point to meet them for coffee or a workout once a week, doing life with them is a good way to get to know a group pretty quickly. Maybe you want to schedule a weekly racquetball tournament or a regular "spa day" when all the girls are welcome to come to your house or office and paint their toenails.

"Finding a time just for the girls was a challenge. We met weekly before youth group on Wednesdays so we didn't take another evening. We had a snack, a short devotion, prayer in two groups (high school and junior high), and then we gave them a bookmark on cardstock with the verse for the week to use in their studies."

—HEATHER ROGERO, VINEYARD ASSEMBLY OF GOD

One summer a friend of mine invited girls from a different grade to come over for lunch each Tuesday. She didn't make anything fancy. In fact, most weeks they had macaroni and cheese. But the girls really looked forward to their lunch date. In fact, they put it on their summer calendars and protected that day. Hanging out with students on a regular basis lets you get to know them more than any elaborate event ever will.

One-on-One

Schedule one-on-one time with your girls, too. You might let them know that certain afternoons are reserved for hanging out with them. Ask your girls to set up times with you when you can meet for coffee or ice cream. While you're with them, make sure they understand that if there's something going on in their lives that they want to talk about, you are happy to listen. Let your girls know that you're accessible to them. You never want to be too busy to meet with a girl who needs to talk.

Be Spontaneous

Maybe you're not one of those naturally free-spirited people. Every hour of your day is planned, and you rarely find time for off-the-cuff stuff. If that's you, you might consider scheduling some open-ended time. As funny as that sounds, if you set aside a few unplanned hours each week to call students and do something spontaneous, it will show them you're available. Call a girl and meet her for shopping or visit her school during lunch if the district allows visitors. Stopping by their lunch periods is a great way to see your girls in their element and also meet their friends.

A wise friend of mine often says, "If you want to be there in the bad times in students' lives, you have to be there in the fun times first." She is the queen of hanging out with her girls. I've rarely seen her turn down a student's invitation to get together. She knows that when they call her, they're probably ready to share something significant. When we're available, we show our students that we care.

One youth minister I know, Donna, told her girls she was going to build a tree house. This particular church had some land it let her use; but I'm guessing that even if it hadn't, she would have found a church member who would let them borrow some land. Each Saturday afternoon she and a small group of girls sawed, hammered, and sweated together. She admits that at first she didn't know if the girls would like doing some-

Julie, a girls' minister, gave me this great idea. She made it known to the girls in her youth group that she would be at a coffee shop at 6 a.m. each Tuesday. Girls could meet her for a small tourney of the fast-paced card game Nerts. Even though it was early, each Tuesday morning a select group of girls would come to see if they could beat her. Most mornings they just played and laughed, but there were days when girls came with serious problems to confide in her. The time spent laughing together had opened the door for a more personal ministry. If you can't do mornings, you can still designate a different time of day when you'll be at a coffee shop each week. Your girls will love dropping in, and most likely they'll grab a few friends for you to meet as well. You can tell them about activities taking place at the church, and you may even get the chance to share the gospel with them.

thing so physical. But as the weeks went on, the group grew to seven. The girls loved the challenge. It wasn't a traditional "girl activity," but it really struck a chord with some of her girls. And apparently they built quite an impressive tree house; after the boys saw it, they decided to attempt one of their own!

Donna explained to me that in the time they spent building together, several of the girls shared some things they'd never talked about with anyone before. Working with your girls toward a common goal, even something as carefree as a tree house, can foster relationships like nothing else.

During exam week you may want to pack little "study bags" for the girls. You could give them each a highlighter, a piece of fruit, some candy, bottled water, and a little note. Although each bag could be relatively inexpensive, it would be a tangible reminder that you know and care about what is going on in their personal lives. If possible, drop the bags off at their homes. This is a great way to meet their parents and find out a little bit about their lives. Stay just long enough to visit for a few minutes and see the girls' rooms, if they ask you to.

The Art of Listening

In our sound-byte world, many have forgotten about the fine art of listening. Despite all the noise, the words, the e-mails, and calls, it seems we really hear less and less. At church events it's sometimes hard to go more than surface-deep in any conversation. That's why it's vital that you set aside time to listen to your girls. When someone is talking to you, do you really focus on her and listen? Or are you constantly thinking about greeting that visitor, making an announcement, or setting up for the event?

Granted, there are things that have to be done. You can't always stand there and listen to one girl talk while never making contact with anyone else. But sometimes God opens a door in a conversation—and you need to clue in. Sadly, I think I miss these opportunities all the time. So often I have the agenda set in my head for how something is going to happen, and I miss what God has put in front of me—an opportunity to really listen to someone. That's why it's important to always be listening to him first. When we're in tune with God, we're less likely to miss out on these opportunities.

Listening Time
Do you schedule time with your girls when you can really listen to them? Make it a point to do things that promote conversation. Take them with you to workout. If you have to make a long drive somewhere, invite a girl to go with you. Offer to give girls a ride if they need one. You have a driver's license, and you're not their mom, so they'll probably take you up on the offer. Meet them for ice cream or a soda after school. If you provide them with time to share, they will eventually do it.

Listening Skills
How are your listening skills? Would your girls say that you really hear what they're telling you? Or do you talk more than you listen? Are you able to discern what's behind your girls' questions? When they come to you for advice, ask God to help you see what they are really asking. Often the things they wonder about will reveal what's going on inside. Let their questions help you get to the core of the issue.

Are you quick to give them answers when what they really need is a sympathetic ear? Of course, sometimes it's necessary to share God's wisdom with them; but other times, girls just need to be heard. The more your girls feel you care about what's going on with them, the deeper their sense of trust will be.

Details, Details

Do you remember the little details about their lives? When they share something personal with you, do you follow up with them later to see how they're doing? Take every opportunity you can to genuinely encourage girls. Make certain that you have a connection point with each one so you can start a conversation with her about her life. And remember, if you're just starting out in a new ministry, be patient—relationships take time to build.

Listening with Questions

How are you at asking questions? Are your questions easily answered with a yes or no, or do they require more? Are you bold with your questions? Make sure your girls know it's okay to be real with you. Once you've built a relationship with a girl, don't be afraid to ask her how she's *really* doing. Ask her how she's getting along spiritually, in her family life, and in her personal life. (Don't assume that all your girls are okay.) There's a good chance that she wants to share much more with you, but she doesn't know how to start the conversation. When you ask good questions, you're opening the door for her.

Referrals

Know your limitations in advising students. If you're not a licensed professional counselor, you'll need to refer girls dealing with more serious issues to someone who is. If you're in doubt about whether or not you should refer someone, be safe and talk to a professional about the situation. If your church has a counselor on staff, refer girls to this person. If not, you'll want to find someone else who can help them. It's a good idea to keep a list of the names and contact numbers of Christian counselors whom you know and trust. Talk to them ahead of time and ask if they'd be willing to be "on call" or readily available when situations with students arise. These situations are inevitable, after all, and we must be prepared.

It's important to note that at some point, at least one girl will tell you about an abusive situation she's experienced—in the present or the past. Statistically, a large number of students in most youth groups have encountered some form of abuse from either a family member or an acquaintance. So it's a good idea to have a plan in place for when a student shares this kind of news with you. (If you've worked in a student ministry program for very long, it's likely you've already heard this from several students.)

Remember: The law requires you to report any abuse or suspected abuse to the proper legal authorities. If a student talks to you about hurting herself or someone else, you must report this as well. Train everyone who works with your youth to be alert to situations like these. You may ask a trauma counselor, legal authority, or your church counselor to teach youth workers what to watch for in terms of the warning signs of abuse.

But above all, especially when you're in doubt about what to do after a student shares something serious with you, you should talk to your supervisor first.

Let Them In

A woman I know swears that when you let students into your home, you open a door for the relationship to go deeper. It's when they see you wearing no makeup and dealing with your dog that they can feel more comfortable opening up to you. In those situations they will view you as real and approachable. While it may not always be possible, it's a treat for girls to see you in your element.

Consider inviting girls over for a meal. It doesn't have to be fancy. You could serve PB&J with ice cream. While the nutrition would be questionable, you can be sure they would enjoy the company. Why not order pizza and ask each girl to bring a few dollars to chip in for it? If you're really energetic, you could have some girls sleep over. Or you could just invite a group over and let the girls pick a recipe to make together. They could even help you with the shopping and preparation. While most girls wouldn't think of helping out in the kitchen at home, they will love helping you in your kitchen. You could have them come over for s'mores, games, Bible study, or whatever you and your girls dream up. The conversation will automatically be more personal when girls feel welcomed into your home. Not only will they love to be with you, but you will get to know them better as well.

When girls have been in your home, they will feel more comfortable calling you or coming by if they have an urgent need. Conversely, if they've never seen the "real you," they won't feel as though they can call you whenever they have problems. The more you build relationships with them, the more they'll feel comfortable talking with you about anything. While you need to strike a balance between ministry and personal time, remember that the more you let girls into your world, the more they'll let you into theirs.

...But Set Boundaries

One youth minister let his students know that any time the front porch light is on, it's okay to knock. Otherwise, they should knock only if it's an utter emergency.

Only you know how much time you need away from the ministry (and from students) to be at your best when you're with them. Determine the time you need, and then make sure you take it. If you need a substantial amount of time alone, schedule it. Don't burn yourself out or continually work to the point of exhaustion. Remember to rest and trust in God's timing—not your own. There will always be endless needs. Make sure you follow the example of Jesus by pulling away to recharge. Be as deliberate as you can be in spending quality time with students and spending time alone. Continually pray for God to give you his gift of balance in your life and ministry.

You'll want to set up emotional boundaries as well. Don't allow a student to become dependant on you for her spiritual growth or support. You're not doing her any favors by allowing this. As a matter of fact, it will cripple her and hinder your ministry. While you want to let your girls get to know the real you, and you want to be their friend, remember that you are also their leader. You always need to maintain that fine line between respect and approachability.

Invite Them to Tag Along

If you're like most people in ministry, your days are absolutely stretched to the limit. You can't imagine how you'll fit in time for one more meeting, event, or Bible study. Have you ever thought about just allowing your girls to participate with you in your daily routine? Maybe you have to go to the grocery store or run an errand on the other side of town. Why not call a girl and see if she wants to ride along?

My friend Margaret told me a story about when she and a student were driving to pick up T-shirts for an event. While they were in the car, Margaret gently confronted the girl about her relationship with her mom. At the time, the girl didn't agree with her at all. So they finished their errand and nothing more was said about it. Seven years later, the girl called to let Margaret know that she and her mother were going through counseling to help them deal with their issues. She also said she'd never been able to get their car-ride conversation out of her mind, and she thanked Margaret for speaking the truth in love to her. Before receiving that phone call, Margaret had no idea that their talk had been so significant to this girl. And it may never have occurred if Margaret hadn't made it a point to spend time with this girl and really speak into her life.

Chances are most girls would think it's fun to help you pick out your groceries and run your errands. I know a girls' minister who invites her girls over whenever it's time to clean her apartment. (I don't know why I didn't think of that!) They love to be with her, and cleaning is fun when there's a big group doing it. They get to spend time with her, and she can take care of some of the things she has to do. Take them with you when you "do life." They will get a glimpse of how you live, and you will be subtly mentoring them along the way.

Be Real

Let girls see you for who you are. Don't worry about being "Super Minister"—the perfect woman with all the right answers who's never caught without her lipstick. Your girls need to see that you're real and that you're comfortable being who you are. They have too many plastic role models already. Share your convictions and life lessons with them. Don't be afraid to let them see you be vulnerable. If you have a problem, you don't have to hide it from them. Obviously, you don't want to air your dirty laundry or go into personal details that they don't need to know; but it will encourage them to see that you have problems, too. As a matter of fact, they will watch you more carefully when they know you're going through something difficult. The way you handle adversity will be a pattern they will follow when they encounter problems of their own. God will often use the pain from our past as our greatest ministry tools. As girls get to know you through all sorts of circumstances, they will learn about God's faithfulness in the different seasons of life.

Cautions

Playing Favorites

While you'll always have favorites, you'll never want your girls to know this. You'll naturally be closer to some of the girls and want to meet with them on a regular basis for mentoring. But you also want each girl in your ministry to feel as though she has the same amount of access to you. Girls are perceptive and can pick up on favoritism quickly. Don't let them even suspect it.

Vive La Difference!

Don't be intimidated by girls who aren't like you. Maybe you're a classic tomboy and some of your girls are more girly girls. Pursue relationships with them just as much as you pursue relationships with the girls who are more like you. Find some shared interests and spend time making memories with them, as well as with the girls to whom you are more naturally drawn. You'll find that girls aren't so much looking for someone to be just like them as they're looking for meaningful connections.

Watch Out for Sarcasm

While your humor style may have a slightly sarcastic edge, this often comes across as rude and cutting. Younger girls especially may not realize you're joking. Instead, they may think you're picking on them. Of course, you want to be yourself; just make sure that when you're joking around, it doesn't translate as rudeness.

Value Being over Doing

Be certain your girls know that you love them for who they are, not for what they do. Margaret, a girls' minister in Kentucky, constantly reinforces this idea with her girls. She reminds them that she values them because of their intrinsic worth, not because of how they perform. She says that this is especially crucial with girls who are leaders. Because they will partner with you and be more involved in the ministry, you need to let them know you love them even when they aren't perfect. They will mess up. Just like everyone else, they will let you down. Make sure they know that if and when that happens, they can still come to you, and you won't reject them.

Make Investments

Continually pray for wisdom about which girls to invest in more deeply. You can't know each girl intimately, so you need discernment about which relationships God would have you focus on most intently. This may change from season to season. Just because you were closely involved in one girl's life in the winter, that doesn't mean you will be in the spring. Some girls may need a little more attention from time to time. As you seek God, you'll receive guidance and wisdom as to where he wants you to invest.

Don't wait for the girls to come to you. Pursue relationships with them. They may be too shy, or they may not take the initiative to get to know you. But you can take steps to know them. Whatever you do, don't sit back. Get out there and get to know your girls. Keep relationships the priority of all you do, and the rest will flow from there.

chapter four

Leading Leaders: Equipping Others to Do the Work of Ministry

Certainly you have a list of Sunday school teachers and volunteers, but do you know who the real leaders in your youth group are? They're the girls who set the tone and then look back to see the others following them. If you're wise, you'll make it a priority to find out who they are. Discovering and utilizing these leaders will do two things: First, it will make your job easier. They can share some of the load of leading the group in the direction God has given you. Next, when they serve within the youth group, their leadership gifts will be nurtured.

Of course, this isn't to say that you should spend all of your time with a certain type of girl in the youth group—the "star material." Some of your leaders may not be the most obvious choices, so make sure you look for girls who show a willingness to serve. When you pour into the girls who are leaders, they can turn around and invest in those who are following them. The younger girls in your ministry will always look up to the older ones. Why not point out to the older girls that they are being watched and followed? In serving the younger ones, they can learn what it means to let God use them in another person's life.

Consider Establishing a Girls' Council

A good friend of mine who's the girls' minister at a large church in Houston came up with this great idea. In getting to know the girls in the youth group, she discovered that many of them had creative ideas for the girls' ministry. So she decided to form a girls' council. This group of girls was elected by their peers to work alongside the girls' minister in planning, praying for, and preparing for events. The girls not only helped my friend minister more effectively, but they also saw firsthand some of the work that's required behind the scenes.

In deciding who's going to be on the girls' council, it's important to stress that it's not a popularity contest. Encourage your group to vote for those who are serious in their walks with God and who desire to serve others in the youth group. You could go through the nomination and election process however you feel would work best for your girls.

My friend introduced the idea of a girls' council during slumber parties she organized for each grade level. There, she set forth the responsibilities of the girls' council and asked the girls to pray about whom they would recommend. She talked about the characteristics of a Proverbs 31 woman and then asked the girls to nominate someone based on that standard. The nomination forms asked the question, "What do you see in this person that reflects the characteristics of Christ?" After a week or so, girls anonymously turned in their nominations, and later all the girls voted by secret ballot. The Christmas after the girls were elected to the council, my friend gave each of them a framed compilation of the things that were written about them during the election process.

You could divide up the number of girls from each grade however you want. My friend decided to choose four students from grade 7 and another four students each from grades 9 through 11. She then chose five 8th graders, and any 12th grader who wanted to serve on the council was also welcome. With this division, the 8th and 12th graders were given a louder voice (more voting power) because they were the oldest students from middle school and high school. The 6th graders had to wait until the next year to serve on the council, as their first year in the ministry was designed to be a time for them to receive. (Note: My friend threw these pajama parties during the summer before the 6th graders were promoted into the youth group so they wouldn't feel left out.) Another girls' minister in Dallas chooses council girls from each of the different schools represented in the youth group. These ideas worked for them, but you should organize your council however it will best fit your group.

You can meet with the girls' council as often as you think necessary. There could be weekly, biweekly, or monthly meetings. You may also want to schedule meetings as the need arises. In my friend's youth group, before her girls begin their yearlong service on the council, they must sign a covenant that explains what is required of them.

In some ways the girls' council will represent the girls' group as a whole. They will help you keep a finger on the pulse of the girls—who are all different ages and attend a variety of schools. As the council meets to pray and plan, you'll get to know the girls better and learn about their culture as well.

Staying "In Tune"

Although forming and organizing a girls' council takes some work, you will immediately start to notice many benefits. You will be "in touch" with the girls of your youth ministry by listening to the council members share their thoughts and ideas. The girls on this council will help you track the general feelings, strengths, and weaknesses in the ministry. As you well know, many times the best ideas for events and Bible study topics come not from adult leaders, but from girls. Not only are they in tune with their generation, but they also tend to have fresh walks with God, which causes them to see things in new ways.

Digging Deeper

You may want to go through a Bible study with them or have them take turns teaching a lesson each week. You could randomly call on them to share what God is showing them in their time alone with him. Another possibility would be memorizing Scripture together. Chrissie requires that her council read through *The One Year Bible* together. At each meeting, she encourages the girls to share what God is teaching them through their reading. She listens to see if they are where they need to be spiritually in order to serve.

Outreach

You could ask some of the girls on the council to follow up with any youth group girls who've been absent. They could design a system for calling or e-mailing the girls to let them know they were missed. One church I know of has a group of girls who call themselves the "Love Squad." They visit students who've missed three Sundays or more. For instance, they may drop by a girl's house in their "Love Squad" shirts and leave her a candy bar. Thus she gets the benefit of knowing that others notice when she's absent, and they receive the joy that comes from investing in someone else's life.

Encourage the girls on your council to always look for visitors at church events. Teach them a few simple questions that will help put others at ease and make them feel welcome. Train them to always be aware of anyone sitting by herself and to be

sensitive to those who are new. You may also want to put your girls' council in charge of following up with visitors. They could call, send them notes or e-mails, or even take a few friends along and go visit them.

Chrissie has her girls send a letter to any visitors on Monday, make calls on Tuesday, and then drop by for visits on Wednesday. The next week the girls will call the visitors again to let them know what's going on in the youth ministry. You will probably want to follow up with the visitors as well—but as you know, contact from someone their age is more likely to make them want to come back.

Learning Ministry

Perhaps the very best benefit from establishing a girls' council is that the girls who participate discover what it means to do ministry. They will see some of the planning that goes into making an event take place. Also, girls who never would have met (because of their age difference) will pray together and have the opportunity to serve one another. Furthermore, they'll learn how to work together toward a common goal. Serving on the girls' council will show them that a leadership position isn't necessarily all glamour; it often means doing a lot of hard work that no one ever sees.

As you meet with these girls, you're really training them to be servant leaders. They may not realize it, but because of your investment, they will be more equipped for ministering to others in the future. Many of them may want to come back and serve as summer interns after they've graduated. And because of the relationships they've formed with the younger girls on the council, they will most likely have a personal interest in the ministry even after they're no longer a part of it.

Event Planning

You can utilize your girls' council to share the load. The girls can help design T-shirts, make phone calls, enlist volunteers, organize prayer teams, and promote events to the youth group and other girls in the community. They can staple, write thank-you notes, run errands, set up rooms, and follow up with visitors.

Feedback

A girls' council is also a great "sounding board" for your ideas. Council members will represent the greater voice of the girls in your youth group by telling you if an idea hits home with them or not. Their input can be invaluable. While you, along with the youth staff, will make the final decisions, make sure you listen to the thoughts and ideas of the girls' council.

Ownership

The more opportunities you give these girls to serve and lead, the more ownership they'll take in the ministry—which is what you want. You want them to view the ministry as "theirs"—not yours or the church's. You want them to pray and serve as if it's their responsibility—because it is. The more ownership the girls take for what's going on in their youth group, the more they'll grow and learn about ministering to others. This will also help you stay humble by keeping your name off stuff. You'll be multiplying the ministry by investing leadership skills in your girls.

Prayer

At each meeting, make it a priority to pray together for the youth group and other specific situations and events. You'll want to set guidelines for prayer request time so there's no chance of it being ruined by gossip. You may want to limit the requests to personal requests for each girl or even things that directly affect the whole ministry. Margaret tells her girls, "You tell me how I can pray for you directly. I'll pray for you as you pray for those in your life." Girls can be assigned prayer partners so they can pray for one another on a more personal level each day.

My friend Cheryl, along with her girls' council, designed a very cool e-zine that changes each month. It's simply a part of the student ministry Web site, and it's especially designed by and for girls. Cheryl and her girls decide on the different topics and write the articles and special features. Girls can also submit pictures and artwork. Cheryl's ultimate goal is to eventually have the girls design it all while she takes on the role of overseer and editor.

Each month the e-zine features an interview with a college freshman and spotlights the girls' events that are coming up. The site also highlights a devotional written by one of the girls. It's a great way to connect with girls and to let those who are interested flex their creative muscles.

You may want to pair up girls from different grades. It will encourage them to get to know others outside of their comfort zones. Since some girls may not feel at ease praying out loud at first, let them know that not everyone has to do so. If an individual wants to pray silently, that's okay. As you make prayer a priority, the girls will grow in their own personal prayer lives and experience Jesus' power.

They can also discover how to pray together for the girls in the youth group and beyond. You might want to design a system where any youth group girl can send an e-mail to a certain address with the understanding that the girls' council will pray for her. One girl could check the e-mail each day and forward the requests to the rest of the council. Girls could also organize a plan for sending prayer notes to those who are being prayed for. Obviously, you would follow up personally with the most serious concerns.

Service First

It's important to stress to the girls' council that while it's a leadership position, it's first a service position. Girls are never to flaunt their roles, exclude others who aren't on the council, or assume they'll always be on it. It's a privilege that carries with it a high calling—service. You can assign them jobs to do at events or during weekly youth meetings, such as greeting visitors, handing out papers, or simply looking for girls who are alone. Constantly challenge girls to find ways to help, pray for, and encourage others.

Give them tangible assignments and also let them find their own creative ways of developing a heart for service. Before our girls' retreat one year, a group of senior girls decided they wanted to serve the younger girls. They called themselves the "Pink Ladies." They were decked out in head-to-toe pink, and they did everything from carrying the freshman girls' luggage to their rooms to hauling equipment and books for me. These girls chose to become Christlike leaders when they chose to serve.

Recognizing Leadership Gifts

Whenever you recognize that one of your girls has a leadership gift, do all you can to encourage her to use it. Give her the chance to lead among her friends and those younger than she is. That may mean giving her a service or teaching role during an event. Or you may have her work alongside you on a project. Do all you can to develop your girls' leadership gifts and to give them opportunities to step out in the ministry roles that God has for them.

Setting an Example
Also, as you meet with the council, you will be mentoring the girls as they watch you live your life and serve in the ministry in which God has placed you. Your example has the potential to mark them for the rest of their lives.

I remember how one of my former bosses on a youth staff always picked up the trash after every event. Our church had custodians who would come in and clean up even the worst mess, but Mike consistently made their jobs easier. He wouldn't tell his staff or interns to do it. Instead, he started to clean up the mess, which would remind us to do the same. Remember, even though you may be "over" others—whether girls or volunteers—you never want to be too proud to do the behind-the-scenes and often menial tasks. Make it a point to practice servanthood. What better role could you fill?

Volunteers

Have you ever wished you could clone yourself so you could be in several places at once? You could cheer at one girl's volleyball game, advise another girl, and get to know a third over an iced coffee. While cloning is not an option, too many of us choose another option by default. We run ourselves ragged going from one place to the next, trying to be all things to all girls and never being fully present wherever we are. It's a fact of ministry: There are always more needs than one person can handle at any given time. This is why it's crucial that your volunteer base is strong and active. They're not an extension of you—they are the hands, feet, and voice of Christ.

"We have to invest in our adults because the student ministry staff cannot do it all. Our volunteers should tap into the lives of at least two to three students and keep up with them."

—MICHELLE SANDERS, FIRST BAPTIST CHURCH

They're a Must!

Maybe using volunteers has been a negative experience for you in the past. You trusted others, and they didn't come through for you. They completely dropped the ball and left you in a bind. It just takes one time, and we start to grow leery of sharing our responsibilities. But if you don't use volunteers, your ministry will never reach its full potential. The girls in your youth group need to hear from more than one female. They need to see empowered younger and older women who have been given the work of the ministry. It shows them that ministry isn't only for the "elite" who work at the church—it's for everyone.

Who Will Fill These Shoes?

Maybe you need to recruit additional women to serve your girls. If so, where can you look? One of the best places to find willing workers is to tap into the moms of girls in your youth group. Most of them would do almost anything for their daughters, even if it meant staying up all night at a PJ party with 50 other girls. They obviously know what teenage girls are like, and they want to see

the youth ministry meet their daughters' needs. They have a vested interest in seeing that things go well.

Another group to look toward are women who no longer have children at home. You may think these women are out of touch and have "retired" from raising children, but many of them are looking for fresh ways to make a difference. They have extra time on their hands and the wisdom that comes from experience, which is an invaluable asset.

One more place to look for female volunteers is among the college students and young singles in your church. Girls look up to this age group. Because these young women haven't married yet, they aren't like extensions of the teen girls' moms. If a single working female talks about waiting until marriage to have sex, a girl may be more apt to take it seriously than if her mother repeats the same thing again and again. Single women can have a tremendous influence on teenage girls of this generation. Many times singles have more flexible schedules to meet with girls than married women with children. They can attend weekend events and even summer trips if given enough advance notice to rearrange their work schedules.

You will want to make sure the younger female volunteers, such as college students, have the necessary maturity to be role models. Are they ready to be in a position of leadership? If so, then definitely give them a platform to serve your girls. If not, encourage them to plug into the college ministry and wait awhile before they step into a leadership role.

No-Brainers

Obviously, for legal reasons you'll want to screen your volunteers in the way your church requires. But you may want to evaluate them even further. Do they have intimate love affairs with God? Are they women who study the Bible and pray? Do they resist the temptation to gossip and complain? If they're young, do they display maturity in their attitudes and actions? Do they dress and act modestly? Are they the kind of role models you want your girls to copy?

Take the time to hear the testimonies of potential volunteers. Listen to what God is teaching them and find out why they want to work with teenage girls. Is it a desire to meet a personal need—or will they serve out of the overflow of what God is doing in them? Are they women of compassion, truth, and wisdom? Is their speech, dress, and overall lifestyle appropriate?

Building a volunteer base takes time, so practice patience. It may take awhile, but with prayer and diligence, you'll see God build a strong team to work alongside you. Once you get a good, solid group of women in place, give the girls plenty of opportunities to bond with them. Many of the girls will hit it off with just one woman—which is enough. If that one woman continually models a godly lifestyle and invests into this teenage girl, the results will be seen for years to come. I can think back to a few women who poured into me during my teenage years—and I still try to model my life and choices after them. Find women who are interested in leaving an eternal legacy and expose them to your girls as much as possible.

Touching Base

You'll probably want to meet regularly with the women you've chosen to serve in leadership roles with your girls. It's here that you can reconnect, voice concerns, give direction, listen to input, and pray together. Let these women be a sounding board for you. Tell them what you're considering for the days ahead and where you think God is leading you. Ask them if they see any red flags or any ways to improve upon your ideas.

"Lean on She"

Let your volunteers share the load with you. As much as you can, "give away the ministry," as one of my friends used to say. This will be the difference between you staying the course and burning out early. It will also give others opportunities to fulfill the ministry God has called them to. God may intend to use the experiences they gain while serving with you to equip them so that he can move them into other leadership positions. As you partner with them, you are, in many ways, training them. In a sense, you are multiplying yourself into others. When dealing with your volunteers, do you keep that in the front of your mind? Are you able to trust them to do the work God has called all of you to do? If so, you, and those with whom you minister, will reach more girls than you could ever reach alone.

chapter five

Girl Groups

Girls long to get real. They want to share their thoughts and feelings and hear others in their peer group do the same. They want and need to live in community and feel like they have a safe place to be themselves. That's why small groups of girls are often the backbone of a girls' ministry. While coed groups can be good for certain purposes, all-girl groups are special. With just the girls present, they are better able to share the kinds of things they wouldn't discuss in mixed company. They can talk much more openly about their worries, temptations, concerns, hurts, and joys. The distraction of boys is eliminated—for at least an hour or two—and they can fully focus on God.

Determining a Group's Purpose

Before you divide up your girls into a bunch of small groups, you may want to decide on the purposes the groups will serve.

Bible Study Groups

These groups should have a leader who teaches and encourages the girls to study the Bible on their own before coming together to share what God is teaching them through his Word. They can choose a Bible study to go through or simply designate a book of the Bible to study verse-by-verse. The following are topical Bible study ideas you could try with your girls:

- My friend Donna told me that her girls had a desire to dig deep in the Word. So she showed them how to study the original Greek and use reference books. Maybe you want to write a study specifically for your girls' needs. Or due to limited time, you might check out some of the good girls' curricula and Bible studies that are out on the market now. Visit your local Christian bookstore or surf the Internet to find possibilities. You should also ask your girls to give their input and share what appeals to them. In addition, it's a good idea to always have some resources stashed away in your office. These would be books and other resources your girls can borrow either to use on their own or lend to a friend.

- You may want to choose a topic for the girls to study together from a biblical perspective, or you could let the girls decide what they want to learn. A friend of mine taught the different stages of intimacy in a relationship. She talked about how to maintain healthy relationships with guys and how to avoid some of the pitfalls. Her girls loved this topic and learned about drawing boundaries and guarding their hearts. Another youth minister I know taught her girls about the important concept of identity. She says that identity is the root of all other issues, and if you address who girls think they are, it will determine what choices they make for the rest of their lives.

- You might want to take them through a biblical study dealing with how to manage their emotions. Girls are too often controlled by their emotions, or they use them to manipulate others. And some may need to learn how to express them in healthy ways rather than stifling them. A biblical perspective would show how emotions are a gift from God and should be used to honor him, rather than for our own advantage.

- Another idea is to walk girls through the different roles God has placed them in. The group could study one of these roles each session. One week they could learn what God says about

"A personal favorite among New Testament stories is the woman who poured out the alabaster box of perfume on Jesus' feet. The value of the perfume showed that she spent all of her future fortune on Christ. I have talked to girls about what we can pour out on Jesus' feet and have found alabaster boxes and jars to give to them. I asked them to write what is most valuable to them for their future—what they place stock in. That way they can pour out this list of future values and hopes at the feet of Jesus. It's a very visual way to remind us to give all of our dreams to the Dream-maker."

—JANÉE ANGEL

being a daughter; the second week, a student; the next week, a friend; and then an employee, and so forth. As they learn about God's purpose for them in each of these relationships, they can evaluate whether or not they are honoring him in the different areas of their lives.

• What about choosing a popular song to discuss each week? You could ask girls to listen to the song during the week and determine the message it's conveying and where the artist is coming from. Challenge your girls to relate the song to the Bible and decide what parts of the artist's message line up with God's Word and what parts contradict it. This would not only teach girls to critically analyze the messages they receive from their culture, but it would also help them apply the Bible to their everyday lives.

• Donna wanted to teach her girls about worship in a fresh way. She gave each girl six pieces of paper and then played about a minute-and-a-half of a song. While the song played, the girls were invited to express (with words or some form of art) their own personal worship on one of the sheets of paper. When the song ended, they were invited to put the papers away, and then another song would begin. She gave them another minute-and-a-half to respond, then played another song, and so on. When all of the songs were finished, she asked the girls to put their pictures in the center of the circle, and then the group considered them together. She asked questions such as, "What do you notice?" or "How does this make you feel?" She asked her girls to share what they felt as they expressed their worship to God, and she recalls that many of her girls really opened up during the discussion time. Some of them said they felt afraid, exposed, or excited. As they shared, they realized that they all responded to the songs differently. Some interpretations were bright, while others were dark. Some were just words, others only colors; some intricate, and others very scant. She explained that just as everyone drew different pictures, the worship styles in the body of Christ are all unique. She encouraged each girl to take a few pictures home to hang in her room as a reminder to live a life of radical worship.

- Why not make it a priority for your groups to memorize Scripture together? A girls' minister I know chose relatively long passages for her girls to memorize. She started with Psalm 1 and then let the girls choose the next passage. She gave prizes when the girls learned their passages and found out later that they were practicing together in the halls at their school.

- You could even let the girls pick a book on spiritual growth to read

"Rather than going through a book, we brainstormed different ways we could worship God through our lives. We made a list and focused on one idea each week. One week we worshiped him through art, and we each made a collage or painting that expressed our worship of God. Another week we focused on serving together on a community project. One week we kept journals. After the three-month study, our group discussed how we could implement those habits into our daily lives. This experience changed how we defined and expressed worship."

—MICHELLE GRAY, SECOND BAPTIST CHURCH

"Teach your girls about spiritual disciplines. As they put them into practice, they'll build habits from which they'll benefit for the rest of their lives."

—MARGARET DENMAN

together as a "book club." Chrissie in Dallas told me she met with a book club at a local bookstore to do just that. The club even gathered interest from people outside the church. It's less-threatening to invite a non-Christian girl to a neutral location, such as a coffee shop, to discuss a book that relates to life and teen-girl issues. Obviously you want to make sure the book has solid biblical lessons and plenty of spiritual food for thought. There are a lot of great books to pick from. It shouldn't be hard to come up with a list of possibilities from which your group could choose one.

- Putting some thought into knowing your girls and understanding the group dynamics will help you know what questions to ask. What are they struggling with? How can you encourage them in their spiritual lives? Make sure your questions have specific personal applications. If a student answers, "I need to pray more," ask her how and when she'll do it. You may even want to ask someone else in the group to pray for her and hold her accountable. When you contact girls during the week, ask them how they are doing with applying the lesson. This is often a great reminder to them, and it encourages them, too. Spiritual growth is accelerated when we know someone cares.

Accountability Groups

An older girl or adult volunteer can lead these groups. The leader should ask the girls to keep everything that's said confidential to protect the level of safety and honesty within the group. Each person can share areas where they long to see growth in their lives. They can hold one another accountable for how much time they spend with God in prayer and Bible study. Groups may even want to make a list of questions that they go through each week, such as, "How much time did you spend reading God's Word this week?" or "Did you do anything that put you in a tempting situation?" The girls can confide places of temptation and struggle, and then the group members can pray for one another.

It's important that the leader be someone who knows how to guide the group away from "venting" and toward a healthy place of truthful sharing with one another. Accountability groups can literally change girls' lives as they see that they're not alone in their struggles and victories. They learn to shoulder the burdens of others and become more real with one another and, ultimately, with themselves.

Service Groups

There may be a group of girls who all enjoy helping the elderly or teaching young children. Maybe they feel called to evangelism. For these groups, it's important that the leader properly train them and that the parameters are clearly laid out before sending them out to serve. Groups like this teach girls to look for opportunities to share their time and gifts with others. Girls who participate will love the

"The best memories of girls' ministry are when we served together. Whether we were making cards for the elderly, praying for the persecuted, feeding the homeless, or spending time with underprivileged kids, the times together were fun and full of lessons. Loving others together in the name of Christ is the best classroom I know."

—SHAUNA RUSHING

chance to come together with other sisters in Christ and make an investment in someone else's life. These groups will often trigger a lifestyle of service and ministry.

Fun Ideas to Try with a Group

Every now and then, change things up in the small group. If you usually meet at someone's home, you may want to change the location to a coffee shop or park for one week and just talk about life. You could either let girls know that you'll meet somewhere new the next time, or when they arrive, simply transport them to the surprise location. Or one week you may want to alter the format from Bible study to just worship and prayer. Maybe you'll have a potluck dinner where each girl is responsible for bringing something while you provide the main course. They could bring their "favorite dish," and even though the food might not necessarily all go together, it would be fun to sample everyone else's favorites.

Let Them Lead

If you sense that your girls are ready to take on some leadership, let them sign up to teach the lesson on different weeks. You could either help them decide what they want to teach or leave the choice up to them. Encourage girls to choose a topic such as "gossip" or "purity" or a passage of Scripture that means a lot to them. Let them know you will help them if they want you to. This will really challenge your girls, and they'll most likely realize that they enjoy studying the Scripture for themselves. Of course, you'll want to evaluate their readiness, but when you see signs that they're up for it, give it a try.

Left Turns

You may want to surprise the girls one week with a totally different format. You could put a sign on the door instructing them to enter quietly and prayerfully, and then lead them in a time of guided reflection. Or you could invite a surprise guest teacher—your pastor or another church leader. One week you could even meet the girls at the door dressed as the Bible character your group has been studying. Doing something a little different every few weeks will keep girls anticipating and wondering what will happen next.

Perhaps you could get together at one girl's house every now and then for a dinner or dessert that you prepare as a group. Or you may ask a different girl each week to plan a fun activity for everyone. The more your girls get involved in deciding the direction of the group, the more committed they'll be over the long haul.

Scoop Sheet

As girls enter the group, you or the group leader may want to pass out a "Scoop Sheet" that contains different questions the girls can fill out while they wait for the others to arrive. They can work on it before and after the group meets, just so it doesn't cut into study time. You could either give them the same sheet each week or vary the format.

Let girls know that they can be as honest or as "surfacey" as they want to be when they fill it out, but the most important thing you want to know is how to pray for them. The questions on the Scoop Sheet will often reveal what girls don't feel comfortable telling you in person but want you to know about anyway.

As you look over the different sheets each week, you can pray about the girls' individual requests. Even though you, or the leader of that group, may not have had time to talk to each girl in-depth, these sheets provide an avenue to knowing what's going on in their lives.

The following pages offer an example of a Scoop Sheet you can reproduce and use:

Scoop Sheet

Name_____Date_____

1. What was the best thing that happened to you this week?
The worst?

2. How are you doing personally?

3. How is school?

4. How are your relationships with friends? Family?

5. Do you feel as though you are honoring your parents? Explain.

6. How is your time with God going?

7. Are you learning from God's Word?

8. Are you listening to God?

9. Are you praying?

10. Is God teaching you anything? If so, what?

11. Are you memorizing Scripture?

12. How can I specifically pray for you this week?

13. Is there something I need to hold you accountable for and ask you about next week?

14. What's your greatest struggle right now?

15. Is there anything else you'd like me to know?

16. Is there anything I can help you with?

17. I know that you know a lot about Christ, but are you keeping it real?

Randomness and Craziness

You may want to think of some random questions to ask the group each week. There are all kinds of books full of lists of thought-provoking, funny questions your girls will love to consider (such as Youth Specialties' line of Quick Questions books). Or try a crazy game, something they may not have played since they were children. The key is to get them laughing so they feel relaxed. The more comfortable they are at the start of a group, the more likely it is that they'll open up later.

Soul Wash

Just as cars get so dirty and grimy that you can't see the person inside, sometimes as we go through life we begin to feel grubby and old as well. We get bogged down and feel badly about ourselves until we get a good "soul wash."

To host a soul wash, give each girl the opportunity to share something positive about the other girls in the group. Ask them to affirm each other's character traits, rather than just saying something like, "I love your sweater."

Ask them to share their impressions of someone else's strengths. You may even want the girls to write down these affirmations for the receiver to keep. You could pass around sheets of paper with each girl's name written at the top, then let them add their affirmations as the papers come around. You could either give the recipients their sheets that night, or hold on to them for a few months and mail them later. You'd be amazed to know how many girls keep these sheets of paper throughout their whole lives. They will leave this soul wash with a fresh look at the valuable creatures God has designed them to be.

Moms

Ask the girls' moms to give you some input in planning fun things for their daughters to do. They may think of something you never would have. They'll love the chance to hear from you and to know you're thinking about their daughters. You may even make some new friends.

If Boredom Sets In...

Every now and then you'll feel like your group's energy is waning and the girls are growing bored with the general direction the group is taking. Don't panic. This happens to most groups from time to time. When you feel as if your group is "dying," take some time to reevaluate with your girls what purpose your group will serve. Ask them what they would like to do in their group and what they see it accomplishing.

Really listen to them, since the more you hear where they're coming from, the more you'll be able to meet their needs. You might want to change things up for a while. Maybe take two weeks to study the book of James and then another two weeks to pray for non-Christian friends. Then you could get back to whatever you were initially studying. Or just let your girls decide what to do to spice things up. The more they feel as though they've shaped the group, the more ownership they'll take to make it work.

Make sure you do fun stuff with your girls on nights that aren't official Bible study time. Get with them and just laugh and be goofy. My friend Julie recalls that the very best time she spent bonding with her girls was when they all went to buy snacks for an event. She says that after they spent one afternoon being goofy in the car together, they were melded together as a group. Make sure you really take the time to know your girls and hear their hearts. This will make all the difference in how they respond as a small group.

Training Leaders

As you probably know from past experience, some leaders do terrific jobs drawing out members and unifying groups; other leaders let the groups drift without direction. How do you find and train leaders who will bring out the best in the group? Just because someone wants to lead a group of girls (i.e., she is a warm body), you shouldn't automatically assume that's where she should serve. Think through a few questions before you place her in this type of leadership position. A leader can either make or break a group. Make sure your leader falls into the first category.

Listening Versus Speaking

Does she know the delicate balance between listening and speaking? I was once in a group where the leader gave us the answer to every question. She had wonderful insights and knew way more than I did—and more than most of the group, for that matter—but no one else had a chance to share what God was teaching them. As a matter of fact, I think most of us came to resent the fact that she talked so much. When looking at a potential leader, ask yourself if she connects with girls. Can girls relate to her? Does she teach God's Word and not merely human opinion?

The Mentor System

One idea is to always have the leader of a group be "training" another leader to come after her. You could pair existing leaders with those who want to become leaders. That way, the "trainee" gets to see a group in action. She could become acquainted with some of the girls and lead different aspects of the group time, such as prayer requests or discussion questions. As she feels more comfortable, one week she could lead the whole group. This is a good way to ease volunteers into leadership, rather than just throwing them into a new responsibility. They can learn with the safety net of having someone more experienced sitting next to them.

Lead the Leaders

It's important that you don't try to lead every group. If you lead the leaders, they will lead the girls. It's a good idea to meet with your leaders on a regular basis to check in with them and encourage them. You may want to ask a volunteer to serve as an encourager for the group leaders. She could write them notes of support and serve them in whatever ways they need. She could also coordinate the prayer requests of the leaders so they all know how to pray for each other.

Two-by-Two

I am convinced that much of discipleship takes place one-on-one—over a long period of time. Just recently I cleaned out some boxes and found many saved letters that older women in our church had written to me over the years. Most of them were from when I was in high school and college, and others were from my early years of marriage. These women invested in me, prayed for me, admonished me, and turned my eyes toward Scripture. They constantly modeled to me what it meant to walk with God. Now years later, I strive to do just that each day.

Maybe you can recall an older woman who took a special interest in you. It could have been a relative or a friend of the family. Maybe it was a Sunday school teacher or neighbor. Whoever she is, thank God for her today. When she looked at you, she didn't see just the young girl you were at the time; she also saw the future you would one day realize. She saw you through the eyes of faith that only God can give.

The word *mentor* is thrown around in many circles today, but the truest sense of the word comes when someone invests in another person for the purposes of God's kingdom. The Paul/Timothy relationship is a tender one. Most people will be blessed to have only a handful of mentors in one lifetime. Why not give this precious gift to the girls in your youth group?

Kelly began a mentoring program at her church recently. She wanted to bridge the gap between the age groups and also offer up older role models to the younger girls. She chose different high school girls to mentor the junior high girls. Basically she contacted these older girls and explained what their role would be, should they choose to accept it. She let them think about it and get back to her if they were interested. If they wanted to participate, she sent them a package in the mail that contained the lists of responsibilities and moral standards, as well as a description of what it means to be a mentor. She also included an RSVP card they were to return to her if they wanted to attend the "Mentor Soiree" held for all new mentors. She said this special little touch built excitement for the girls, and they loved receiving an actual piece of mail.

At the soiree event, Kelly talked about her own experiences of being mentored and mentoring others. She emphasized the impact they could have on someone else. She gave each high school girl a little book that had the name of their junior high girl on it, along with mentoring ideas, descriptions, quotes, and other helpful information. As it stands, the program is set up so that the junior high girls don't officially know that they have mentors. The high school girl is responsible for seeking out this younger girl and building a relationship with her. Kelly said some of the older girls are really taking the initiative to make that connection, and others have held back a bit more. Once this initial round of pairs gets going, Kelly will partner up more girls to begin the mentoring relationship.

Retreat Mentoring

You may want to give older girls opportunities for mentoring during retreats and events. For instance, on one retreat Cheryl gave the senior girls various leadership responsibilities. After sessions she announced that senior girls would be available to talk to any younger girl wanting advice. Cheryl had previously coached the seniors on listening and even leading someone to Christ. They were told that if they were in doubt as to what to say or if any situation that a younger girl shared with them was serious or life threatening, they should get Cheryl or another youth worker to intervene. She said it was amazing how many girls went to the seniors to talk and pray. They knew these girls

would understand what they were dealing with, and they felt comfortable sharing their concerns and problems with them.

Seniors were also given the role of offering "cabin talks" at the end of the night. They were divided up among the cabins and shared a short devotional about what God was teaching them.

A Night on the Town

Invite mature juniors and seniors—and younger girls—along with some adult sponsors to come. Then divide the girls into groups with at least one sponsor and one older girl in each. Next send your girls out (with the sponsor driving the small group). Encourage them to go bowling, play games, or go out to eat. It's a great way for older girls to invest in the younger ones, and for the middle school girls to get a close-up look at those whom they admire and emulate.

Summer Groups

If your church arranges for college students to work with you over the summer, encourage each one to find a small group of girls—or even just one girl—whom she can focus on over the summer. Let her take a few weeks to find a group she clicks with, and once she does, have her take intentional steps to mentor this student or small group. Some of these relationships may last well into the school year and beyond. What's more, the ripples of their influence may be seen for years to come.

Women at Church

Another way you could match up mentors would be to ask women in your church if they would mentor your girls. You could appeal to different ages in their Sunday school classes and have

them fill out questionnaires. Then you could match girls who want mentors with women who want to mentor someone.

You could designate a curriculum for each pair to go through or give them the freedom to choose their own study. Determine what you feel comfortable with and then communicate that to the leaders. You may ask them to meet in person, e-mail each other, or speak by phone a certain number of times a month. Or you could just leave it up to the pair to decide. If you want to use a more informal approach, you can simply encourage them to meet for sharing and prayer.

The girl and her mentor might even have a desire to serve together in some capacity. If so, they could consider working at a soup kitchen, teaching young children, or helping an elderly woman in her home. As you know, the girls will learn more from being around these women of God than from hearing 1,000 sermons. Life change will take place as the girls see these older women as people whom they can emulate.

Whatever the format, the purposes should be building relationships and spiritual encouragement. Advise them to plan activities where conversation is the focus. They might want to get ice cream, play miniature golf, or meet at one of their homes. At the kick-off meeting or party, share about the purpose of mentors. You could teach about Naomi and Ruth or Paul and Timothy. Be sure to stress that the goal is life change and developing godly character. Encourage those who enter into such a relationship to take it very seriously, with the mindset that this could turn into a lifetime relationship.

As much as you possibly can, partner with the women's ministry leader at your church or whomever has the most consistent contact with women. That may be the pastor's wife, a volunteer, or a woman on staff. Share with her your vision for your girls and ask her to come alongside you in any way she can. She may be able to help you find volunteers when you need them. You might even team up with her in planning one or two events a year where the women and girls come together.

If Nothing Else...

If you don't want to set up an official mentoring program with your girls, make sure you talk with them about the importance of finding mentors. Explain the role of mentors and give them some tips on what to look for in finding them. Challenge your girls to seek women they respect and who live their lives to honor God. You might want to roleplay a conversation of how they might ask an older woman to mentor them. Help your girls open their eyes to the potential mentors all around them.

It's Your Job, Too!

While encouraging others to mentor girls is wonderful, it's vital that you also focus on mentoring. You will need to determine, with God's help, how many girls he wants you to focus on at one time. A friend of mine says that at any given time you can only mentor three girls one-on-one. For you it may be fewer than that, or it may be more. However many girls you mentor, make sure you pass the mentoring mindset along to them as well. Instill in them the importance of pouring life into someone else. Each girl you mentor should also be mentoring a girl younger than she is. Ideally it would be incredible to see a ministry

where every woman and girl was matched with someone older and someone younger. The ripple effects would be amazing, as females—young and old—pour into one another.

Don't wait for girls to ask you to mentor them. Pray for wisdom and then pursue the girls whom God puts on your heart. Many girls have the need and desire for mentoring relationships, but they don't know how to ask. They may be too shy to take the initiative, but they will jump at the chance if you offer it.

Mentoring Pointer #1

Margaret wrote down her goals for the girls on a chart and prayed over them each day. She listed each girl's name, what she wanted her to learn, what change in her life she prayed would happen, and what steps Margaret was going to take to help each girl accomplish that goal. It was a great reminder for her to keep that purpose in the forefront of her mind whenever she interacted with a girl or prayed with her or for her. Even if you don't have a target like this, you're still being helpful. But in some ways, you're just putting out fires. Setting an aim for each girl you mentor will help you make the greatest impact.

When you spend time with a girl you're mentoring, be deliberate in every aspect. Let your overarching purpose guide where you go, what you talk about, and even what kind of things you do when you aren't officially "meeting." Even when you're just hanging out, be certain that the time is intentional. If you want to get together with her just to have fun, then make sure you have a really great time. If it's to talk, provide an atmosphere where conversation can flow easily. Think ahead about the kinds of questions you'll ask and how you can challenge or encourage this girl in her walk with Christ.

Before you meet, pray for God to provide teachable moments. And then when they occur, be prepared to make the most of them. When you're talking with a girl for the purpose of holding her accountable, keep in mind a mental checklist of questions you intend to ask her. Of course, you'll want to leave room for the Holy Spirit, but before you meet with a girl you're mentoring for any length of time, have your purpose in mind.

Mentoring Pointer #2

When you're with a girl one-on-one, don't be afraid to ask her the hard questions. Ask her if she's applying what she's been learning in Bible study. Ask her how you can pray for her—and then pray, right then and there. Follow up with her on anything she's shared with you before. Encourage her to keep growing in the spiritual disciplines that will build her faith muscles. Lovingly confront her when you feel you need to. If you sense you need to talk with a girl about an action or attitude, then prayerfully speak with her. The goal of mentoring is for girls to grow in maturity in their walks with Christ.

Don't be afraid to challenge your girls to take their faith to the next level. Talk about what God is teaching you and then relate that to how they can trust God in every detail of their own lives. Emphasize how God wants to use them in their worlds to make a difference and to introduce others to him. Remind them that the Holy Spirit will give them the power to live the Christian life the more they rely on him. Most importantly, make sure you focus your relationship with them on Christ—not on yourself. The goal is for girls to become "independently dependant on Christ."

A girls' minister I know started to build a relationship with a girl in her church. In their small group Bible study, whenever this girl would write down her prayer requests, my friend could never quite decipher them. Over time, she began to realize that the girl couldn't read. My friend immediately investigated her situation and found out that she was home-schooled, but she wasn't

getting adequate attention to learn. She set the girl up with a tutor from their church, and over time the family decided to enroll her in public school. While she was drastically behind the other students in her class, she was very excited that she was learning to read and write.

Several people from the church agreed to pour into this student. A high school girl (whom the girls' minister was mentoring) agreed to meet with her. They got together to study, exercise, and volunteer at the youth office. Overall, this older girl was instrumental in helping her develop life skills. Even the older girl's family got involved in...

Mentoring Pointer #3

Memorizing scripture is another great activity to do together. Both of you will use it for the rest of your lives. It's easier to stay committed when two people are working on it together, and it certainly makes it more fun. Choose a passage, chapter, or book together, and make a realistic plan to memorize it. You'll be amazed at how much a girl will love doing this with you.

Mentoring Pointer #4

When choosing the girls you want to invest in, don't overlook those who seem quiet or passive. It's so easy to focus on the girls in our ministries who give back to us and who readily flex their leadership muscles. But we must constantly be aware of those who need our help. These girls often have much more time to spend with you, and the encouragement they receive from you will mean the world to them. You may be one of the only constants in their lives. Make time to go places with them, take them to lunch, and share life skills.

Mentoring Pointer #5

While you'll always want to mentor girls, it's a great idea to also mentor a younger woman who works with you in the ministry. Maybe there is a college or seminary student with a heart for girls. Make it a point to include her as you minister. Take her with you when you visit girls. Give her plenty of opportunities to serve—in private and public ways. Teach her what you're doing and why. Pray with her and answer her questions. You may even wish to share in a time of Bible study each week.

As you serve her, you are multiplying yourself. Not only will your girls have another role model, but you'll also be helping to train up someone else in ministry who may be there after you're gone. The more we share the work God has given us, the more we give others the opportunities to develop and use their gifts.

...the mentoring. The mother helped her shop for school clothes, and the father tutored her in various subjects. An art teacher also took a special interest in her and helped her discover that she had a special talent for art. This girl now has her artwork displayed in a gallery in New York City.

She not only learned about God from the women of the church, but she also learned about developing the basic skills that she needed to succeed in life. By showing her how to read and write, they were meeting her needs. In ministering to her cognitive and social needs, they received a platform to speak into her life about her spiritual needs. Mentoring is sharing what we have received—in Jesus' name.

Mixing and Matching

Chrissie in Dallas gave me this wonderful idea—she said that once a month, she goes through the youth group roster and randomly picks 12 girls, two from each grade. She then sends each of them a pretty invitation to a dinner party at her home and asks them to RSVP. She and a team of girls from the church shop for and cook a simple meal. They set the table and prepare for this dinner, which they call "Table for Twelve."

She said that when the girls arrive, they are very quiet, as most of them don't know the other girls. She stands back and watches the "hostesses" (those who helped her prepare the meal) introduce the girls and get the conversations started. In about 10 minutes, they're all enjoying themselves and each other.

These dinners give girls the chance to get to know others from their youth group who aren't in the same grade or school while also getting to know the girls' minister better. Many times the conversations take on a spiritual tone, and girls are given the opportunity to open up in this more intimate setting.

chapter six

Events

As much as girls love being with boys, there is something special about gathering without the boys around. During those times, girls seem freer to be themselves and have fewer inhibitions and masks. For this reason it's a good idea to plan events especially for your girls. They can be as elaborate or as simple as you want. Many of the ideas in this chapter can be adapted for a group of two or a gathering of 200. Let these ideas spark your own creativity in planning fun and meaningful events for your girls. The possibilities are endless, as are the different personalities of the girls in your group.

Know Your Group

Each group of girls will take on its own persona. What will work for a small church may not work for a larger one. That's why it's crucial that you know your girls. The more you learn about them, the easier it will be to plan creative events they'll enjoy. Know what they like, what they're interested in, and where they are in their spiritual walks. Spend as much time with your girls as you can. Make it a point to call them regularly, work out with them, or just do life together. If you need to run some errands, why not grab a girl or two to go with you? Or if you are doing tedious work at the church, like addressing envelopes or sorting curriculum, invite them to help you. As their hands get to working, their mouths will start moving.

The best way to think of events your girls will enjoy is to let them in on the planning process. When they plan it, they will take ownership of the whole event—and of course, you know it'll be something they like to do. For one-time events, you can take some chances. If something doesn't go over, you can always try a different idea next time. So let your creative juices flow.

Promotion

If your girls are like most, their schedules are often maxed out—so the sooner they know about something, the better your chances they'll attend. And the more times they hear about an event, the more it will stick in their minds. That's why publicity for your events is crucial. Whatever you do, don't overlook the important work of promotion.

A girls' minister I know always mails "Save the Date" cards when she's planning a special event for her girls. She has told them to put these cards in a place where they can see them and let them serve as a reminder to pray for the event. When she started sending these cards, attendance jumped for most events. Sometimes it helps to cut your cards a little differently as well. If your brochures are usually designed one way, why not change the size and style from time to time?

As much as you can make your event stand out from whatever else you've done in the past, girls will take more interest. For some events you may not even want to give the full details. Sometimes a teaser line will pique their curiosity. You may just want to give them a hint of what the night will be about—just enough to grab their attention.

The best way to promote an event is to ask girls to promote it themselves. This is a perfect way to enlist your girls' council, if you have one. Ask them to make phone calls, send e-mails,

put up posters, and visit Sunday school classes and Bible study groups to talk about the event. When girls hear that their peers are excited about what's going on, they will be much more apt to sign up and attend.

Once-a-Month Gatherings

It's a good idea to bring your girls together every now and then for corporate worship and teaching. While small groups are essential, there's something inspiring about gathering girls of all ages for a special event where you can address topics that are of particular interest to girls only.

Chrissie told me about their once-a-month, girl-only meeting called "GLO," which stands for "Girls Living Out-loud." The goal is to let the Word of God sink deep into the girls' hearts where it will change their attitudes and actions. Each month she brings in a different speaker, and her girls' council helps her decide on the topics. One night they talked about gossip; another night they discussed modesty. For the latter, she simply promoted it as "How to Keep a Secret." The girls had no idea what the talk would be about, and it created a lot of interest and buzz. They brought their friends with them to see what was going to happen. Chrissie said that girls still talk about this night because it really hit home with them.

Another month Chrissie brought in a Christian nutritionist to talk with her girls about dieting, healthy eating habits, and eating disorders. She labeled the talk "Instructions for Living in Barbie's World." The girls had a lot of questions, and it was a great way for them to learn relevant information for their friends and for themselves. The nutritionist then used the Bible to talk about how God had specially created each one of them. She encouraged the girls to see themselves through the loving eyes of God.

Topic nights such as these are great for drawing in girls who wouldn't necessarily come to something titled "Bible Study." You could advertise in schools and in the community about what you will be doing at your once-a-month meetings.

For another one of the GLO nights, Chrissie asked a panel of mothers and daughters to answer questions before the group. In essence, she had them share their stories. She invited a mother and daughter whose husband/father had died, a pair from a blended family, two who had dealt with an eating disorder—mothers and daughters with all sorts of stories. By sharing their testimonies, they showed girls that they could deal with anything if they relied upon God. From listening to these stories of endurance and victory, the girls received the gift of hope.

Another good idea is to host an event that offers a "Guys' Panel." If you tell a girl she'll have an opportunity to hear what's going on in a male's mind, you can bet she'll jump at the chance. That's why you may want to ask a panel of guys to speak to your girls every now and then. You'll probably want to meet with the guys beforehand to prepare them for what to expect. You could allow girls to ask them questions right on the spot, or you may want to ask the girls to write their questions ahead of time so the guys can prepare. This is probably the best way to assure that their answers will be thorough and Bible-based. Ask the guys to use a passage of Scripture or a biblical principle when they respond to each question.

Michelle, a girls' minister in Houston, plans a once-a-month Saturday gathering for her girls called "Framework." Each month they discuss a different aspect of the Proverbs 31 woman. Michelle says the goal is to allow God to change them as they work on the frame of becoming a girl with a biblical backing. First they do a creative activity, and then she shares a short devotional. Michelle focuses on one central theme at each gathering and plans an activity to reinforce that theme. Girls feel comfortable bringing their friends along, and they look forward to seeing what she will plan for them each month.

One month they had a paint-your-own-pottery store provide picture frames for the girls to paint. Then she shared Psalm 139 with them and talked about how the girls are each "fearfully and wonderfully made." Another month she invited an aerobics instructor to come. After a short workout, the girls learned about honoring God with their bodies. At another gathering she asked hair and makeup experts to give a few makeovers, and then the group discussed inner and outward beauty.

They also plan service projects from time to time. During the Christmas season, they went to a home for senior citizens and later discussed the compassionate side of a Proverbs 31 woman. They also participate annually with Operation Christmas Child by filling shoeboxes with small gifts for children in need overseas. One year they even made beaded necklaces to put in each of the gift boxes.

I heard about another group that enjoys "Grab a Mug" nights. Girls pay $5 to attend. As they walk into the room that night, each girl grabs a mug and fills it up with one of the provided beverages. Then they share in a night of worship, complete with candles and a guest worship leader. If you wanted to do something similar with your group, you could ask volunteers in your church to provide the drinks or even the mugs.

Some girls may want to plan a sports night, where they get together to play an organized sport, such as softball or soccer. Others may want to attend a play or do crafts. Still others may enjoy planning a fancy dinner. Don't be afraid to try all kinds of activities with your girls. You'll know which ones they love and which ones you should rethink for next time. The point isn't how elaborate the activities are; it's that the girls are together and sharing.

Weekly Events

I recently heard about a group of girls who started to meet once a week at 6 a.m. for Bible study and prayer. They named their time together "Thirsty," based on the dictionary definition of the word. They call themselves "eager, craving, and parched," as the word suggests, and they meet for a short time of Bible study led by a different girl each week. The girls take turns sharing what God is teaching them at home or at school, and the girls' minister simply facilitates the time, giving leadership when necessary. For those who can't make the meeting, the girl who leads the study then posts a summary of her talk on the Thirsty blog.

Another group meets after school on Mondays for "Work It." The girls get together to do Tae Bo and share a short devotional time afterward. Someone discusses a biblical view on how to take care of the body and use it for God's service, rather than using it to draw attention. They've also discussed healthy eating habits, rather than the extremes. Nutritious snacks are provided, and they've even printed T-shirts to get the word out to other girls. Each week the girls memorize a verse that talks about using our bodies for God's service, and they are encouraged to share the previous week's verse as they enter the room the next week. Girls from area schools have started to come, and their weekly group is growing.

I heard of another group that offers weekly "Pilates and Lattes," where girls meet once a week for Pilates and then head to a coffee shop to "cool down." Girls can come to one or both parts, and while they are having coffee, someone shares an encouraging talk. You may want to arrange to host the workout time at a non-church location so girls who don't attend your church might be more apt to check it out.

Fun Ideas

- Sarah planned a night called "In-Tents" with her girls. They camped on the church property and showed a movie on the side of the church. It had an old-fashioned, drive-in feel to it, and the male volunteers took care of the movie and the security. It was something different and a good way for girls to invite their friends to the church in a non-threatening environment.

- You could invite your girls to sleep over in your backyard. Everyone could sleep in tents—a fun way to host without the mess of having the girls in your house all night. It would also have the feel of camping out, but with the luxury of nearby bathrooms and showers. Give each of your girls a "job" for the night. Different girls could plan the food, entertainment, games, supplies, and even the schedule.

- Why not plan a "movie character dinner"? Tell the girls they can dress up like any movie character they choose. Then give prizes for the most creative, best dressed, and funniest. I heard of one girl who dressed in gray and painted her face and arms gray so she looked like the star of a black-and-white movie.

- One group planned an annual Chocolate Festival. Girls and moms all brought chocolate desserts, and they overloaded on sugar for the night. Everyone voted for her favorite dessert, and the winner received a prize. Girls are already looking forward to the next festival, and some of them are planning new recipes with their moms.

- How about planning a "Girls' Survival Day," where you ask different people from your church to teach your girls a variety of life skills? You could have someone show them how to change a tire, how to balance their checkbooks, or how to plant a tree. Be as creative as you want and get your girls' parents involved. They will be glad to have their girls learning new things while they're also having fun with their friends. This is another great way to reach out to girls in the community, too.

- Plan a brunch where your girls can come eat and hear some insights from a women's panel. You could assemble women from your church's congregation, who walk with God and have a heart for students. Ask them to be ready to answer questions from your girls, and then invite the girls and women to come to someone's house for the brunch. You could even ask everyone to wear PJs so the event has a more relaxed feel. The women could take a few moments to share their testimonies, and then the girls could ask any questions they wanted. Not only will they get some of their questions answered, but they'll also get better acquainted with godly older women with whom they can build relationships.

  Or ask some of the older girls to serve on a panel where they answer the questions of the younger girls in the youth group. Julie hosted a time like this called "Lessons from the Bottom of the Coffee Cup." The older girls shared what they wished they would have done differently. Many of them discussed things they had learned about friendships, boys, school, or God. They talked about the lessons they learned from the youth group, their families, and their friends. It was a great night, and the younger girls, as well as the older ones, want to do something like it again.

- Why not plan a "Pamper Day" with your girls? Ask the people in your church who sell makeup and other beauty products if they would be interested in using them to serve your girls. You could send girls from house to house to see and sample the different products. They could even receive free makeovers or try samples of fun foods at each location. While the girls may not buy a lot, it's still free advertising for the sellers who participate.

- Kelly in Oklahoma planned a daylong retreat where girls could come and relax while learning about who they are in Christ. She divided the girls into different groups, and then had them rotate through the various sessions she had planned for them. One session was on fashion, where college girls majoring in fashion design and a woman who worked in the industry taught about trends and modesty. In another session a college student and a married woman taught about dating and sexual purity. They shared their testimonies and what they had learned, then welcomed questions from the girls. Groups also rotated through a fun session where they talked about hair and makeup with professionals in those fields. They showed the girls new styles and let them practice giving each other makeovers. The girls had a blast getting and giving new looks. At the end of this time, the leader wrapped it up by talking about God's definition of beauty.

In groups about food and nutrition, the girls discussed taking care of their bodies without becoming overly focused on them. They also went to a session on exercise and dance, where the girls had a great time cutting up with their friends. One of the sessions explored encouragement, and the leader showed the girls how the simple act of doing a "little thing" for someone else could make a huge impact. She talked about the biblical definition of the word *encouragement* and then gave the girls opportunities to write notes of encouragement to others who may be having hard times.

If you decide to plan an event like this, ask your girls to help you decide the topics for the day. A speaker could be brought in at the end of the event to tie all of the sessions together in her closing talk. It might also be a good idea to offer one "free-time" session where the girls could do whatever they want: Hang out with their friends, check out the resources, or spend some time alone. Using volunteers would keep your costs down, and of course, the more you get donated, the less you have to buy.

• A friend of mine planned an event for her girls called "Tickle Me Pink." She invited an image consultant to talk to the girls about choosing the right style of clothes for their particular figures. She then taught them about what it means to find their identities in Christ in a world that constantly tells us to do otherwise.

• Why not plan a "Silly Supper"? Invite a few students to come over for a dinner that will keep them guessing. You might even dress up like a waitress and really ham it up. Print out a menu that labels every food with a foreign name and the utensils with a number. When girls arrive, have them order two names and one number for each course. They won't know what they're ordering and may request their dessert and salad first, or only a drink. Let them know that whatever they order for each course is what they will eat. They might have to eat their dessert with knives or their meat with spoons. When all of the courses are finished, students will have eaten all of the food, but each person will have had her meal in her own particular order. It's a fun way to mix together girls who don't know each other and let them laugh and visit in a relaxed environment. You may want to do this with your girls' council or even a small group of new girls.

Special Occasions

Holidays are a great time to plan events for girls. You might schedule a Christmas shopping Saturday or a mini pre-Thanksgiving feast in your home. Or you could do something re-lated to Valentine's Day and remind the girls that their ultimate fulfillment will come from knowing God. While holidays are a busy time for you and your girls, they offer unique opportunities for you to minister. Some girls who may not have healthy home environments might really enjoy the extra attention they receive from you during the holidays. Be sensitive to your girls who have lots of spare time and may be struggling with the "blues" during the season.

"A midnight breakfast with your girls is a great way to bond. I've done this with large and small groups. When it was my small group, I kidnapped my girls, and we headed for the closest 24-hour restaurant, pajamas and all. When the group was larger, we kidnapped in teams and brought them back to the church. Waiting for us were some of our guys having cooked a full breakfast and acting as our servers. In both settings the conversations were great and the memories lasting!"

—AMY JACOBER, AZUSA PACIFIC UNIVERSITY

New Students

Before the school year starts, why not host welcome parties for the new middle school and high school students who will be joining the group? You could use the opportunity to let your oldest middle and high school students lead the planning and promotion. Make it a lot of fun and encourage your older girls to make an effort to talk to the new ones. At the event, you and your girls could share a little bit about the purpose of the ministry and the opportunities they have to get plugged in.

Christmas

During the Christmas season, you may want to invite the 6th graders to participate in a special rite of passage into your ministry. And you could make this event really special for the new girls by encouraging the ones who've participated in the past to keep it a secret. That will ensure that it's a fun surprise for the new girls each Christmas.

Provide the necessary supplies for the girls to decorate some Christmas cookies, and then have a contest where everyone judges the cookies. Set up different categories such as "most festive," "most colorful," "ugliest," and so on. Make sure you have enough categories so everybody wins something. At the end of the contest, have everyone enter a cookie into the "Best in Show" category, then give a prize to the winner.

When the contest is over, preview the upcoming events and share your vision for the girls' ministry. Also make sure you let the 6th graders know how happy you are that they're now part of the ministry. You may want to end the night with a time of singing carols and drinking hot cocoa. If there are any leftover cookies, you could plan to take them to a local senior citizens' home and sing carols with the residents.

If Christmas isn't a good time for your group to do something like this, you could adapt the idea and try it during a different holiday. Have the girls dye and decorate Easter eggs for an egg coloring contest instead, then give the eggs to a children's egg hunt.

Valentine's Day

My friend Beverly hosted a "Pretty in Pink" party at her home one Valentine's Day. She decorated with pink flowers, ribbons, and candles, and each girl brought a bouquet of her favorite flowers. They spread out all the flowers in her laundry room, and then each girl was able to create a custom bouquet to take home.

After sharing a brief devotional about the beauty God sees in each of us, she gave everyone a card with a miniature wedding dress on it and the words from Isaiah 61:10: "I delight greatly in the Lord; my soul rejoices in my God. For he has clothed me with garments of salvation and arrayed me in a robe of righteousness, as a bridegroom adorns his head like a priest, and as a bride

At the party Julie planned for her middle school students, she asked for four volunteers. These girls were then taken to another room for an hour, while high school girls made them over. They did their hair and makeup and then brought the middle school girls back to show the group. The whole group was given a chance to share what they liked about the girls' new looks. After they commented on the outside stuff, Julie opened up the discussion to talk about inner qualities. She said that it was so neat to hear the girls affirm their friends. Then the high school girls who'd made them over were given the chance to say something. They basically just spoke truth into these girls' lives while the middle school girls hung on every word they said.

adorns herself with her jewels." Each girl left with the knowledge that she is the beautiful and cherished bride of Christ. The girls loved taking home the bouquets as tangible reminders of the gift of love God lavished upon them.

Easter

I heard of one girls' minister who invited a woman to share about how communion is like a Jewish wedding ceremony. Girls were served communion and then given time to meditate on the death and resurrection of Christ. They were encouraged to wear white and to invite their parents. After the ceremony concluded, there was a reception complete with cake and party food. Some of the parents gave their girls a small gift to remind them of a memorable time in their walks with Christ.

Prom Season

It's fun to host a pre-prom party where girls can come for free manicures or pedicures (given by volunteers). Or you could plan a party for a few weeks after the prom, where the girls wear their formals and go do something together.

One group planned an event called "Flippin' Formals," where the girls got decked out in their prom dresses and flip-flops and just hung out. You could also call your event "Girls' Prom" and all go out for pizza, a scavenger hunt, and bowling. If someone in your church has a fun car or even a limousine, you might see if that person is willing to chauffeur the group for the night. Girls will love an excuse to wear their dresses again, and they'll look forward to just goofing off with their girlfriends. You may also want to ask someone to be on hand for fun photo opportunities, as everyone will love having their pictures taken with their friends all dressed up.

(Important note: Before you organize events like these, consider the feelings of any girls—even if it's just one girl—who may not have gone to prom.)

Hard Times

Make it a point to remember the not-so-great times in your girls' lives as well. If one of your girls has suffered the loss of a family member or friend, anniversaries can be especially hard. Check with that girl in the days leading up to the anniversary of her loss. She'll be touched that you remembered and will probably want to talk about how she feels. Even though her friends may have remembered, they might feel uncomfortable bringing it up. Make sure you let your girls know that you are there for them in the good times as well as the bad.

Little Things Mean a Lot

Events can be as big or as small as you want them to be. While it's great to plan fun outings for your girls, don't forget to take advantage of making every day a special occasion. If one of your girls makes the basketball team or wins an award, paint a fun sign and hang it on her front door or decorate her car. Take her for ice cream to celebrate and ask her to invite a few of her friends to come along. Your girls may or may not remember the events, but the special times where you really made an effort to step into their worlds will stick with them for a lifetime.

chapter seven

Let's Get Away: Girls' Retreats

There's something wonderful about getting away from our everyday lives and surroundings and shifting our gaze. While your whole youth group probably gets plenty of opportunities to do this, it's nice for the girls to get away on their own every now and then. When you plan a retreat for your girls, you give them the opportunity to hear from God without the distractions of the world and the opposite sex. Sometimes this may mean a small slumber party; other times it's nice to plan a more elaborate retreat. In this chapter you'll find ideas that span from the simple to the more complex. The great thing about doing a girls' retreat is that depending on your volunteer base, budget, and time allowance, you can tailor it to what works for your group. Make sure to involve your girls in the planning. A friend of mine meets with a group of girls to discuss what they liked and didn't like about the last retreat. Then they brainstorm how to make the next one better. Some of her greatest ideas were born from these conversations with her girls.

"The thing my girls remember most is coming over to my house a couple of times a year for slumber parties. We would stay up late talking, and they loved having my undivided attention."

—BETH ANNE DANE

PJ Parties

I know what you're thinking—you can't stay up all night anymore. I hear you! But you might consider reinventing this old standby activity and using it to build community within your group.

Cheryl, a girls' minister in Houston, decided to call these divided-by-grade sleepovers "It's a Girl!" parties. She bought decorations that read, "It's a Girl!" and put them everywhere. She made publicity posters and fliers with this theme and posted them for the girls to see. When the girls arrived at the slumber party, they were greeted with a bunch of activities designed especially for them. They painted their toenails, played word games, watched a clean "chick flick," and ate lots of chocolate. They could enter the "Best PJ Contest" or the karaoke lineup. She didn't have to spend a lot of money getting ready. The women in the church made desserts and brought nail polishes. She held her slumber parties in the church, but you could also try a centrally located house.

Cheryl divided the girls into small groups so they could get to know others they wouldn't usually talk to during youth group. For the younger girls' parties, she asked godly older girls to come and help. An older girl stayed with each group throughout the night. She then had all of the groups rotate through different "stations" where various activities were planned. The stations were in different areas, and she even designated a place where girls could sleep when they needed to. While some girls were painting their nails, others played games. Every hour but three was filled with activities for the girls. As the hours ticked away, they moved from place to place and got to know each other in different contexts. Girls were free to be themselves and competition seemed to melt away as boys were no longer in the picture.

Everything she planned for them had a purpose. As they painted their toes, someone talked to them about having "beautiful feet" and sharing the gospel with those who hadn't heard it (Isaiah 52:7). At another station they learned about different service opportunities that would be available to them that year. As Cheryl did, it's a good idea to spotlight the ministries your

church offers. Invite women to share about the various ways girls can serve. You could also offer information about upcoming mission opportunities the girls can be a part of. Whenever possible, seek to plug them into the broader ministry of the church.

Toward the beginning of the night, Cheryl led an interactive Bible study on a topic that interested the girls. Then—together—they chose a theme verse for their grade. All of the girls were given the opportunity to give their input before voting for the verse that best conveyed the group's heart. And they all worked together to memorize it. Cheryl also asked the girls what they wanted for the ministry. She listened more than she talked, as the girls were ready to share their thoughts and ideas about what would work and what were the biggest needs of their group.

After each slumber party, Cheryl compiled what the girls had shared and e-mailed the list to all of them. In the e-mail, she reminded them that this was their ministry and that they were just as responsible for what happened throughout the year as she was. Cheryl said these nights not only brought them together physically and emotionally, but they also brought them together spiritually.

Retreat Ideas

Vogue

Alissa found vintage *Vogue* magazine covers to use in her retreat promotion. She printed on her fliers, "You cannot afford to miss Vogue." Since this retreat was before Christmas, she even designed cards that read "All I want for Christmas is to go to Vogue." When girls purchased these cards for someone, it represented a ticket to the weekend. Students gave them to their friends, and parents bought them for their daughters. It was a neat way for girls to invite their friends and get the word out. Alissa also gave out a prize to the girl who brought the most visitors, and she said she was surprised by how many people her girls invited.

Before the retreat Alissa visited all the Sunday school classes and asked the girls to write down the top three questions they would ask a guy. She then picked the most common questions and asked guys to answer them on camera for a cool video she planned to show during the retreat. Some of the girls were shocked by the guys' answers—especially the guys from their very own church.

Alissa also asked the youth pastor to write a letter to the girls about the worth of women. In it he talked about how valuable women—and these young women in particular—are to God. At one point during the retreat, the girls' minister read the letter and talked about each girl's worth to her Creator God.

When girls arrived at the church on Friday night, there were large, vintage *Vogue* posters displayed everywhere, and women stood like posed mannequins all around the room. The music was pumping and a fun introductory video played. Creative touches like these often set the tone for a retreat. They let girls know that it's going to be a time full of fun, with tons of surprises.

After the activities were over, girls gathered in groups where they processed what they had heard. Before bed, the sponsors led a talkback time using questions based on that night's teaching. The girls then spent the night in the church. (If it isn't possible for everyone to stay at the church, host homes would work just as well.)

Saturday morning started the "Day of Beauty." A local salon gave complimentary makeovers to several girls. All of the girls were able to get their makeup and nails done, and at least 30 girls received free haircuts. Alissa asked a few local stores if they would provide the clothes for one of the sessions that included a fashion show. They were happy to do it since it was free advertising for them.

At one point the girls' minister stood up to share her heart with the girls. Toward the end of her talk, the lights went low as she read them a letter she'd received that week. It talked about how much the sender loved her, treasured her, and enjoyed being with her. Many of the girls cried and were moved by the tender words. She then revealed that the letter was from Jesus and that it told how he felt for each girl in the room. When they looked under their chairs, they found the same letter hand-written for each of them. She says that out of all the feedback she received regarding that weekend, girls commented the most on how much that letter impacted them.

One woman shared about the importance of nurturing the mother/daughter relationship. She talked about some common pitfalls to guard against and some ways to grow a positive and open connection. Girls were then challenged to prayerfully evaluate whether there were some changes they needed to make or steps toward reconciliation they should take with their own mothers. They were then given time to reflect, call their mothers, or talk with an adult.

On Saturday afternoon Alissa spent about an hour with the seniors, while the rest of the girls had a time of play and pampering. She shared about the importance of letting God use them to make a difference in their families, their schools, and their world. (If you wanted to go more in-depth, you could also use a spiritual gift inventory to help girls determine their spiritual gifts.)

The retreat lasted Friday night through Saturday afternoon, and it cost each girl $25 to attend. There were times when the tone was serious, and other times when the agenda was fun. Alissa's team of volunteers received more than 50 items donated from church members and local stores to give away as door prizes. At the end of the afternoon, a lip-sync contest gave everyone the chance to just let loose. It was fun for the girls to feel the freedom to sing and dance and express themselves. Alissa said girls are still talking about this event, and many of them want to bring friends the next time they do something like this.

Bring It

During one retreat I heard about, girls studied about putting on the full armor of God and then learned self-defense from a local law enforcement official. During this retreat, there were "soak times" (when girls learned and received) and "squeeze times" (when girls gave and served). They simply went to a camp and enjoyed roughing it and spending time talking by a campfire late at night.

For Mothers and Daughters

A mother-daughter retreat is another good idea for a getaway. Plan sessions for moms and daughters to attend separately and then together as well as activities where moms and daughters serve each other. They could give each other pedicures, or daughters could cook together and serve their moms dinner. (It's a good idea to invite some "stand-in" moms for girls whose mothers can't be there, for whatever reason.) Moms will enjoy seeing what happens in the girls' ministry, and daughters will thrive on making new memories with their mothers.

Homegrown Wisdom

You don't have to bring in fancy speakers or musicians to have a retreat that your girls will love. Ask the women in your church to lead and serve. You probably know women who have incredible relationships with God and who have much to share about walking with him. Ask one of these women to teach. If you know someone who has an amazing testimony about her younger years, give her the platform. If you have a real ham in your church, ask her to dress up as a funny character and lead morning aerobics to wake up the girls. You may even want to record the sessions so that those who would like to hear certain talks again would have that option, or they could also give the tape or CD to a struggling friend.

Location, Location, Location

Be creative as to where you'll have your retreat. You may want to check out local hotels for competitive rates or retreat centers and camps. Maybe someone in your church owns a lake house they would let you use. You can stay in town or leave, depending

on your timeframe and budget. Also check out the girls' confer-
ences that come to your area. They can be a great way to offer
something for your girls without a lot of planning on your part.
While you'll be with girls from other churches for the group sessions, you can individualize the time alone with your girls at
host homes or the hotel.

If you want to keep the cost down for a retreat, it's a good
idea to utilize your church building. Girls can stay in homes
overnight and then come to the church for group activities and
sessions. Bring in women from your church to teach the sessions, or invite girls' ministers you know to teach for you, in
exchange for you doing the same thing for them later. You may
want to ask a church member or even a team of older girls to
lead worship at a retreat.

"Build Your Own Retreat"

One year our girls could choose from all kinds of electives taught
by different godly women. Some went to the talk on body image
and eating disorders, while others were interested in witnessing.
There were groups such as "What Does God Say about Dating?"
dealing with wounds from the past, how to study your Bible, getting the most out of your quiet time, prayer, missions, dealing
with depression, and a group on "What to Do When Bad Things
Happen" that had standing room only. The more choices the girls
have, the better chance they have of hearing something they really need to know or remember for this season of their lives.

You may want to divide the girls into smaller "family" groups
for the extent of a retreat. You could give each group the name of a
singing group, or whatever creative idea you and your girls dream

Joy, a girls' minister, offered four sessions at her girls' retreat. She asked different women to teach each session. One woman talked about self-image and related that to the story of Esther. Someone else discussed dating and shared her experience of waiting for and meeting her husband. Another woman talked about prayer and showed girls how to use a prayer journal that a team of women at the church had put together just for the girls. One woman showed girls the nuts and bolts of having a quiet time. She brought examples of different books and taught about practical ideas she had tried in the past.

For the finale of the retreat, girls went into a candlelit room with just their Bibles and prayer journals.

They spent quiet time praying about all God had showed them throughout the weekend, and then they quietly walked out to go home. As girls left, a volunteer handed them goodie bags and handwritten notes from the volunteers.

Women from the church helped with every aspect of this retreat, from the speaking, to the music, to the food. Because of their service, Joy was able to keep the costs down while offering the girls a fun and meaningful retreat.

up. Small groups provide girls with the personal touch of a leader and the chance to process what they're learning. And it's also a great idea to write discussion questions based on the talks they'll hear, so the leaders can use them with their family groups.

A S.O.L.O. Retreat

Julie shared the concept of a S.O.L.O. retreat with me. She and her husband take their students on a retreat where they learn how to spend time alone with God. It's very intensive, so they only invite older students and plan it over a long weekend. They take 12 students and give them a few guidelines before they leave. Students are to leave cell phones, games, watches, clocks, radios, drinks, and snacks at home. They come with very little—just a few personal items and their Bibles. On Friday afternoon as the retreat begins, they start their fast. They are not to eat, can drink only water, and when they get to a certain point in their van ride, they're asked not to speak.

When they arrive at their destination, they watch *The Passion of the Christ* in silence by candlelight. At the end of the film, students are asked to journal their thoughts—in total silence—in the S.O.L.O. journal they received when they arrived. Next, they have a short time of sharing, and then students go to bed in silence.

On Saturday morning they are awakened early and asked to keep their silence. Each student receives an apple, and then they are sent out to spend the morning alone with God. When all the students are brought back to the retreat area, they eat lunch together in silence—it's just crackers, cheese, carrots, and water. After everyone finishes, it's time to take a nap, which they will all need after their intense morning. When they awaken, they're sent out for a 45-minute solitary walk, during which the leader makes dinner for everyone. During dinner they cannot eat unless someone serves them. The leader asks questions about the day, such as, "What was your struggle today?" or "How did you hear from God?" When dinner is over, they play music and light some candles. Each student is given a canvas and paints and is encouraged to create out of the overflow of her experience of the day. When each girl finishes, she's asked to go to bed without disturbing the others.

Sunday is a much less intense day. After breakfast students are encouraged to go for a walk for a few hours alone. When they return, everyone plays games outside. The day is pretty much open for creating, resting, reading, journaling, or praying. Students can spend the rest of the day with one another or alone if they choose. When they awaken on Monday, they share a prayer time and a big breakfast. They play some more outside games, and on the way home they stop at a special restaurant to debrief and laugh. Students are encouraged to keep most of the details of the retreat to themselves so they don't spoil it for others who will attend later.

While the S.O.L.O. retreat isn't necessarily a "fun" retreat, in many ways it's the most important student ministry event they will attend. Here they learn about the practice of spending time alone with God without the distractions of the world. These few days will mark them for the rest of their lives. Sure, there are hard parts to the retreat, but they will probably hear from God in ways they never have before. For most of them, this retreat is the most time they will have ever spent alone with Jesus.

Other Ideas

Girls' retreats don't have to be all fashion shows and makeovers. You can offer a wide variety of activities for your girls. Your athletic girls might want to engage in some physical activity while on the retreat. You may want to organize a football game or let them think up their own entertainment.

Other girls may be interested in art. Why not invite a local artist to teach the girls some fundamentals and then let them create something? A friend of mine designated a "creativity room" and let girls go in at different times during the day to paint pottery and canvases or make bags. If girls are willing, some of their paintings could be displayed in the youth rooms at the church.

"Start a running club where you go no faster than the slowest runner. It's a great way to emphasize health without having to be one of the super athletes. You'll also get to spend time building relationships with your girls."

—AMY JACOBER, AZUSA PACIFIC UNIVERSITY

They could even express creativity by making collages. Give them some magazines and let them cut out words or pictures of things that describe who they are. You may even want to provide girls with a sketch of a "paper doll" and have them give her a new image. Or you could ask someone to teach your girls about using art to worship.

Others may have an interest in dance. Why not invite someone to teach girls the art of interpretive dance? One retreat I know of has worship dancers who tastefully offer interpretation during the corporate worship time. They also feature an artist onstage who paints on a large canvas during the worship. Trying different things brings a fresh element to a retreat. Listen to your girls. Hear what their interests are. They'll bring you some of your best ideas.

"Plant a community garden with your girls. Have them seek a space and work the soil. Encourage them to each take a patch while enlisting community members to do the same. Share the results."

—AMY JACOBER, AZUSA PACIFIC UNIVERSITY

How about planning a retreat for just your seniors? Keep what you're doing a secret until the retreat starts. Use the time with them to really challenge them about where they are spiritually. Spend individual time with each girl to listen to her concerns, victories, and goals. Ask family and friends to write the girls letters and give them to you ahead of time. Then while the seniors are at the retreat, give them their letters wrapped up with a ribbon and encourage them to spend time alone reading them. You may also want to speak a blessing over each girl, sharing what you see in her and how you envision God using her in the future. Girls will remember these words for the rest of their lives.

Technical Details

Delegate

The more people you have helping you, the more fresh ideas and hands you'll have, along with more free time to spend with the girls. Divide tasks and assign them to your volunteers. The more you do this, the more you are giving the ministry away. You're allowing others the opportunity to use the gifts God has given them to bless the Body.

One Woman, One Job

I have always found it helpful to ask a different woman to head up each particular aspect of the retreat. A volunteer might be the head of the food team or the decorations team. If you find one person to be in charge of an area of work, then she can enlist people to assist her. She can also bring girls in to help her as well. My general rule was "find one woman to head up a team and have her partner with one girl." The woman would recruit her peers to help on that team and the girl would find hers. Girls were subtly mentored as they worked toward a common goal with the women on their teams. This arrangement allows the girls not only to learn about serving, but also to build relationships with godly older women.

Designate a woman to lead the prayer team. Ask her to gather a group of intercessors that will pray for you and all who are leading at the retreat. Give them the names of the girls as they register and ask them to sign up for times to pray as the retreat occurs, even throughout the night. The prayer warriors don't have to be members of the student ministry volunteer base; they can come from throughout the church. They can be recruited from the pulpit, in the bulletin, in Sunday school classes, or in Bible studies.

Ask another woman to head up the decorations team. Of course, you'll want to give her a budget and some direction—and then let her create. For some retreats I was a part of, no money was available to purchase decorations so the women brought things from their homes. My friend Kristin transformed a stark stage into a girl's trendy bedroom by simply using favorite accessories from her house and my office. When girls entered the room, they were immediately drawn to the amazing stage that instantly let them know this was going to be a fun weekend. They even used it for a backdrop for the pictures they took with their friends. You've probably already thought of that certain someone in your church who has just the right mix of creativity and resourcefulness to decorate in style and within your budget. If so, ask her for help—then prepare to be wowed!

I asked another volunteer to head up the hospitality team. She gathered door prizes and goodie bags for the girls. For months in advance of the retreat, she went to local businesses with a letter printed on church letterhead asking for donated items. You wouldn't believe the things we received to give away! There were free haircuts, candy apples, CDs, accessories, and all kinds of fun things for the girls to take home. She wrote to some ministries asking them for extra girls' magazines and books, and the boxes started arriving in the mail. Her team of women put bunches of little gifts in bags for the girls to open once they arrived at the retreat.

This woman also organized a cookie drive at the church. She asked 10 women to each ask 10 more women to bake homemade cookies and deliver them to the church. The cookies poured in, and she and her team sorted and put them into plastic mini-bags. It was a great way to get the whole church involved and to give the girls a special treat as they arrived.

Her team also made handwritten notes that went into the goodie bags that each girl received. One week before the retreat, she asked some senior girls and volunteers to come to her house for a time of snacks and writing notes. They added a Bible verse and a quick note encouraging the girls to really listen to God over the weekend. I know some of the girls still have the notes they received at a retreat eight years ago.

You may want to ask a woman to be in charge of resources for the weekend. She might sell a few books, devotionals, or CDs that you think would be beneficial for your girls. Most of the time you can talk with your local Christian bookstore, and they will provide you with the items to sell on consignment. Girls are more apt to pick up something they can use in their quiet time after experiencing a great weekend with God.

Another woman could head up the late-night activities. She might put on a variety or talent show where girls could perform in groups or individually. They could sing, dance, perform a skit, or use whatever talents they have. There could be funny prizes for each participant rather than winners or losers. There could also be a late-night pampering option. This woman and her team could be responsible for everything from planning to finding the necessary equipment. She might also ask someone on her team to take pictures of the girls throughout the weekend and make copies for them to keep afterward.

Finding Volunteers

You may want to check in with different women's groups in your church and appeal for help. Call a girl's mother and ask if she would like to head up a team with her daughter. One year I even held a small luncheon where I described every volunteer opportunity and asked women to sign up that afternoon. You could also pass out cards to your existing volunteer base, asking them to commit to the weekend and check an area where they might be interested in helping.

Special events can also offer opportunities for the men of the church to support the girls' ministry. You would be amazed at how excited they will be to serve. One year when our retreat had grown to a substantial size and I knew we were going to need a lot more help than in the past, I shared our need with the chairman of the deacons. He ran my request by the men on the board, and they were thrilled to serve in any way they could. They signed up for different shifts to help load things and to help girls find the different breakout rooms. And they also helped the girls get to and from their cars—with all of their stuff—in an absolute downpour. They were our "security team," and their faces beamed as they carried luggage and assisted girls. Our girls loved seeing their fathers and grandfathers standing around in their camouflage shirts as both overseers and servants. Later a deacon told me that the weekend was just what the board had needed to unify them in purpose once again.

Tangible Reminders

A friend of mine believes that if you give a girl a tangible reminder of an important event or decision, that item will be a keepsake of what God did in her life. For instance, one summer she found inexpensive flip-flops at a discount store. She bought various sizes and colors and had them printed with the girls' ministry logo and verse. When girls wear those shoes, they are reminded of how God moved in them that summer. Another woman had journals printed up by her church. Girls used them for note taking at the retreat and later had them for their quiet times.

One time my friend gave each girl a little charm with a blossom on it. It reminded them that they were blooming into God's women. Many of those girls still wear their charms, and some will keep them for the rest of their lives. Several Web sites carry sterling silver charms at competitive prices. Remember: You don't have to spend a lot of money; just be creative. You can print stickers with cool logos or sayings right from your computer. Girls will love putting them on their notebooks and school stuff. Or get decals printed for their cars. If you shop around, you can find decal shops that are willing to print them for competitive prices.

Ask local stores to make donations or ask people in your church to "sponsor" these giveaways. Maybe you could even make something for them or print bookmarks, notepads, or calendars at your church. One girls' minister asked a team of volunteers to make her girls "book thongs"—cord or rope bookmarks with beads on them. They were fairly inexpensive, and her girls use them to this day.

Alissa asked a team of girls to make flower pens for her Vogue retreat. She put them in pots on each table to serve as the centerpieces. They used floral tape, silk flowers from a craft shop, and ribbon to put together these funky pens. Girls used them to take notes during the retreat and then took them home as reminders of what a great weekend they had with God.

Another idea is putting together a collection of devotionals for your girls. You could ask youth leaders, staff members, college girls, moms, and even your friends to write some of the entries. Give the writers a sample entry and some suggested topics. You may want to assign what they write about, or just give them the freedom to decide. After you receive the entries, you'll want to ask a team to help you edit them for grammar and content. You could either have them printed through your church's print shop, if it has one, or send them out to a printer. You could even print them from a computer and tie the pages together with ribbon. The girls will enjoy reading about the experiences of people they know, and they'll learn something from the life lessons shared. The things you give them need not be elaborate. Just find something that will spark a memory when they see it. Let your imagination run wild—and of course, use your girls' great ideas, too.

chapter eight

Stepping Out: Reaching the Community

While your first priority is the group of girls God has given you, it's all too easy to forget the thousands of other girls in your area who need Christ, as well as Christian girls who aren't a part of your youth group. Once you've established your girls' ministry, ask God if there are girls outside your church whom you're also supposed to reach out to and disciple.

Use Your Talents

Consider offering to lead a class or seminar for a local club or school in your community. Think of whatever your area of expertise is and be creative as to how to teach it to a group. You could offer a course on hiking, poetry, or cooking. You might even teach free guitar lessons—assuming you can play, that is. You could design the class to be a one-day seminar or a weekly series. Your talents and experiences can be a great outreach tool.

When you do something like this outside the church walls, you'll meet a whole new group of students. Many schools would be excited to have someone in the community take an interest. Obviously you'll be required to go through their background check process, but even though this may take more time than you wish, it's worth it. Just by making this simple investment in the community, you'll gain social capital you may need down the road. These groups will know that you care about students (beyond the ones in your own youth group) and that you can be a valuable resource should they ever need you.

Partner with Schools

Whenever you possibly can, you'll want to partner with the schools in your area. Introduce yourself to the administration and let them know you're available if they have a need. You never know when something will come up; they may call on you for help. The more they feel you're on their team, the more you'll develop and maintain their level of trust. Of course, you'll want to make sure to respect their guidelines and rules so that you're doing all you can to make their jobs easier.

I've heard of girls' ministers who've regularly served as substitute teachers in their students' schools. It's a great way to become a positive role model in the community, and it will also help you see and better understand what your students go through every day.

An After-School Tutoring Experiment

Cheryl, along with her team, has started a free after-school tutoring program for students in her ministry and the community. She advertised in her local area and has had many students come in for help. Cheryl has given the leadership of the tutoring program to a trusted volunteer who coordinates the tutors, times, and students. Cheryl basically oversees the program and just steps in when an issue arises.

Tutors were recruited from the student ministry workers and the church body, as well as through the volunteer placement program the church offers to all new members and those looking to serve in a ministry.

This simple program has been an incredible outreach tool for Cheryl and her team. Word has spread that this local church offers free tutoring, and the program has grown. Parents and students who don't attend the church have come and been impressed by the level of commitment and care of the tutors. Many students

who've come for tutoring have later come back for a youth ministry event. This is a great example of the church meeting the needs of the community in practical and creative ways. They don't have a "secret agenda"; they just tutor. But in some cases, the doors have been opened for students to meet Christ because willing adults took the time to invest in their lives.

Coach

If you have any athletic skills at all, you have an open door to some amazing girls who are in desperate need of adults in their lives. Consider coaching a team in your area. You may even want to co-coach a team with another adult. It's a great way to meet unchurched girls and make a positive investment in them; just be ready for all of the drama. As you build relationships with the girls on your team, you'll find that they look to you as a role model. They'll ask for your advice on everything from boys to their futures.

Let Your Girls Help You

Utilize the girls in your ministry to reach girls who aren't. Students are better at reaching their friends than we will ever be. Encourage your girls to introduce you to their friends and even their friends' parents. Ask your girls to occasionally invite you to come along when they're hanging out with a group from school. Or simply find out what your girls and their friends like to do for fun and then invite them to get together for that activity. If you have a budget to buy them coffee or lunch, take advantage of that.

Ask the girls in your youth group to give you a platform to serve the groups they're involved with. For instance, if you know several cheerleaders, maybe you could lead a Bible study for the squad before games. This would not only encourage your girls to boldly live out their faith, but it would also give you the chance to meet others who aren't Christians. If you have girls on the track team, offer to help the coach in whatever way you can by simply bringing refreshments to practices or games, making phone calls, or loading equipment. You may even want to provide a light dinner for a particular team before one of their games. Obviously you'll need to make sure that doing this doesn't violate any rules in your school district.

Even if you don't do anything official to support the team, make sure you're a consistent face in the stands by regularly going to the students' games and events. The more you step outside the church walls, the more chances you'll have to meet those who don't know Christ.

The Coffee Shop Experiment

Michelle works at a big church in a major metropolitan area. After school, the students in her city hang out at a local coffee shop. So on any given day, this place is packed with girls drinking their frozen coffee drinks and gossiping. This gave her the idea that every now and then it would be great to offer conversation with a purpose where these girls could receive an encouraging word. She believes that this generation's non-Christian students need a middle ground before they'll set foot in a church. So she started a weekly time for girls to visit after school at the coffee shop, and her youth group girls invited their friends. They also invited any girls who were already hanging out there to participate. Students who would never come to church were happy to talk with her and the girls from the youth group. Since it was a non-threatening place where they felt comfortable, even when the conversation took a spiritual direction, the girls opened up easily. Find out where the girls in your area hang out after school and consider offering them a conversation with purpose every now and then.

In planning for these afternoons at the coffee shop, Michelle invested her time into a few core girls from her youth group. She coached them in how to give a short devotional and ask pointed questions to stir up discussion. In looking back, she recalls that this preparation time for the girls was key in getting them to catch the vision and follow through. She said it really equipped her girls to dive into the lives of their non-Christian friends. The more they prayed and planned for these after-school hangout times, the more ownership they took for reaching their friends in their schools. The girls' minister showed up about once a month to add to the discussion and meet girls. The more time these girls spent visiting with her, the more comfortable they felt around her. Some even called her to get advice about specific problems and situations, and others showed up at girls' events. Still others met Christ because of discussions they had with another student or the girls' minister after school.

Another group made it a point to go to a coffee shop together after their summer Bible studies. They purposely went where they knew students who didn't go to their church would be hanging out. They resisted sitting all huddled together; instead they turned their backs to the tables and faced outward to talk with the other people there. It was a drawing agent for students to come over and talk with them. Some of the curious students even decided to check out the Bible study the next week.

College Students

You may want to utilize some college girls who've already graduated from the student ministry to help you reach out to younger girls in the community. Why not ask a college student to host a Bible study for high school girls in her apartment? Ask the girls in your youth group to invite their friends with the promise that they will get to hear a little about life from the perspective of a college student. What 10th grader doesn't want to hear about the experiences of a college girl? Choose a simple book to discuss and give most of the leadership to the college girls.

Leann tried this idea with her group. She said her girls brought lots of their friends because they loved hanging out with these older, cooler girls. If you choose to offer a study to middle school girls, you could ask a high school girl to open her home and take leadership. This will give you the chance to meet girls in your community while offering others in your youth group opportunities to spread their leadership wings.

Walk in Their Worlds

The more you get to know your girls' friends, the more chances you'll have to make an impact on this generation. When you go to your girls' events, make it a point to meet as many of them as you can. Be casual—you don't have to go through the plan of salvation with them or invite them to all your youth events. Just listen to them and get to know them. Chances are they won't come to your church because you slaved over relaying the details of an event; they'll come because they have a relationship with either you or a girl in your ministry. The more you step into your girls' worlds, the more you'll see God expanding your influence to those outside the church walls.

Chrissie shared with me that for home football games, she asked a volunteer to videotape the drill team's halftime show each week. This volunteer then edits the show and puts together a video of the highlights. The Tuesday morning after the game, she shows the video at a small Bible study at the church. Drill team girls who don't even attend her church come to see the video and hear an encouraging word for their week. By taking this little bit of effort, she has had the chance to serve and love girls who need to hear about Christ.

I heard of a church that offered a quarterly outreach called "The Bridge." The girls handled all of the details of planning and spreading the word among their friends at school. They decorated their youth room with paintings and candles and had a real coffee barrista come in and serve the girls. The coffee and desserts were free, and girls could come share their art, sing a song, or read some of their poetry. Someone played live music, and students hung out and played games. Girls who never would have come to a church service showed up and felt welcomed. Church girls were comfortable bringing their friends to this non-threatening environment, and these nights opened the door for many spiritual conversations.

My friend Margaret opened her home for dinner before every home football game. She made it known to her girls that all they had to do was let her know on the Thursday before if they were coming, so she knew how much food to buy. Each girl brought a few dollars, and many girls brought their friends. The only spiritual thing she had planned was her prayer before the meal. After dinner everyone went to the game together and then spread out, and Margaret introduced herself to her girls' friends. It was a great way to meet girls who wouldn't necessarily come to the church, but who were open to having a relationship with her.

Balance It

Continually pray for a balance of "in-reach" and outreach. Pass along the outreach mentality to your girls. Remind them that God has placed them where they live during this exact moment in history intentionally (Acts 17:26), so he can use them to make a difference. Partner with your girls in ministering to their friends, schools, and community.

chapter nine

The Footsteps of Christ:
Giving Girls Opportunities to Serve

While girls' ministry is great for meeting girls' needs, they in turn must learn how to follow the example of Christ and give themselves away. In our me-centered culture, it's so easy to believe that everything is about us. That's why it's crucial that you offer opportunities for your girls to minister as well. The more they learn to serve others, the less self-absorbed they will be.

Calling All Volunteers!

Maybe you know of a food pantry, orphanage, or hospital close by that could use some good volunteers. I know of one girls' group that goes to a nursing home once a week to give manicures and play games with the residents. Promote these opportunities to your girls, and invite their mothers to come. I've heard of youth groups cleaning out their closets and donating their clothes and jackets to places that give them to the underprivileged. You could take your girls to a home for unwed mothers to hang out with some of the girls there. As they get together to serve, they'll be reminded that the simple things they do can make a difference in someone else's life.

Helping the Homeless

Beth Anne said she'd been looking for a way to get girls out of their bubbles, so she took them to serve with some church members who work with the homeless in their area. On a Saturday morning they went with a group of adults to hand out clothes and bottled water. She said that at first, the girls were a little bit scared, but once they relaxed, they really enjoyed talking with the different people they met. The girls loved the chance to share with those who had so much less than they did. Many of the girls told their friends who didn't go how much they'd missed. So many girls have asked about going back to visit the homeless that they're planning another outing.

Beth Anne shared a poignant story about that day. When they drove up to the parking area, several people who had slept on the nearby lawn the night before were wandering around. As the girls watched out of the van, one of them just blurted out, "Look at all these people! Where do they live?" Naturally, the others explained to her the meaning of the word *homeless*. Her comment is a perfect example of how close we can be to a different world, while at the same time so detached from it.

Crisis Pregnancy

You could take your girls to help out at a crisis pregnancy center in your area. In our town, Saturdays are the busiest day when the center needs the most volunteers. Girls could help sort through donated baby gear, answer the phone, or simply pray while someone is being counseled. Some of the girls who come in for help may be from their own schools. This can open the door for your girls to befriend those who are experiencing a challenging time. Serving in this capacity will start the conversation with your own girls about abstinence, adoption, and abortion. Many of them will have questions for you. As your girls become familiar with the pregnancy center in your area, they will be able to refer girls they know from their school who are looking for alternatives to abortion.

Sports Clinics

Just as your youth group is unique, so are the needs of your particular community. After you identify those needs, give your girls the opportunity to partner with you in meeting them. Beverly and her girls are putting together teams that offer sports clinics in their area. The goal is to reach children who aren't affiliated with a church. The girls will promote a soccer or basketball clinic for a particular Saturday, and then the team of students, along with a few adults, will host the event. Girls will later follow up with the families to see if they are looking for a church home. During the clinics, they plan to teach some basic skills, referee an actual game, serve lunch, and spend some time hanging out with the kids. They will also share a short Bible lesson as the day winds down. It will give these children a connection to a local church and provide some older role models for them. It's a great way for athletic girls—and even those who aren't but want to serve children—to make a contribution to those in their community.

"Some of my girls are very athletic. They love nutrition and exercise. I asked them if they wanted to promote and run a 'Boot Camp' for any girl wanting to participate. They jumped on the idea. We all met at 6 a.m. each weekday for a short devotional followed by a workout. Each week we also memorized a Bible verse the girls chose. It was a fun way to focus on our total health and a good place for girls to bring their friends."

Random Acts of Kindness

Maybe you want to gather your girls to participate in random acts of kindness. Let your girls think of some creative ways to practically and tangibly express God's love to people. You might bake some cookies for those who work at the local fire station and deliver them together. Your group could also shop for a family in need and leave a sack of groceries on their front porch. Or you and your girls could write notes of encouragement and just sign them "Your Sister." Get together with your girls to brainstorm ways to bless others anonymously. The more they participate in random acts of kindness, the more they'll just naturally think of ideas when they're going about their daily routines.

Why not take your girls into the community to give out bottles of water to joggers or wash windows for businesses? A friend of mine is planning to take some of her girls to a park and make breakfast for those who are passing by. She will bring a big package of pancake mix and a griddle and have her girls advertise "free breakfast." You could even go where you know there are people who haven't had a good meal in a long time. It wouldn't cost a lot, but it's a great way to meet needs in a practical way.

"There are a lot of internationals in our community. We offer conversational English classes every day, and they give us opportunities to meet and build relationships with women from all over the world. If you have international families in your area, this is a great way to reach out to women and girls who may not know Christ."

—BEVERLY PARRISH, BAPTIST STUDENT MINISTRY, TEXAS A&M UNIVERSITY

Tutoring

Why not encourage some of your older girls to tutor at a local middle school? Or take them to a school that has an especially large need for role models for their young girls. Of course, you'd want to meet with the administration to share your idea first. If the school agrees, train your girls and give them the general rules they should follow. The students will receive practical help with their schoolwork while building relationships with role models.

Helping Established Ministries

Take time to learn about many ministries already helping people. Some may be across the world, but others will be within miles of your church. Find out what they are doing and give your girls the opportunity to join them. You might want to partner with an organization that specializes in exposing students to missions. Or take your group to help out with a ministry that reaches the homeless in your area. Your girls can help sort clothes, pass out food, or play with children.

You could recruit a group of volunteers to help build a house with Habitat for Humanity. Ask your female volunteers and moms to jump in as well, and make it a special event for everyone to get to know one another. Also girls may want to adopt families with specific needs and partner with a group of women from the church to provide for them.

One group I heard of loaded up their equipment and piled into vans. They drove into a small town that was mainly comprised of elderly people, and as each student got out of the van, the youth workers told them to find their ministry. The students went from house to house asking people how they could help. They simply looked for ways to serve and share with people about Christ. So often we provide students with their ministry rather than trusting God to lead them to it. As students "created their ministry," they had to decide where God was leading them. By the end of the day, students had connected with the residents so much that some residents even invited the girls into their homes for dinner. Girls had done everything imaginable, from painting to repairing and construction to simply listening to stories from the past. From this one day, many of them have gained new eyes to see opportunities for serving others all around them.

Christmas

Christmas is a great time to help a family by providing them with gifts for their children and fun things such as a Christmas tree, decorations, and a turkey. If you have a lot of girls interested in doing this, you may want to divide them into groups, with a different one assigned to each family.

"Talk with your girls about being created in the image of God, and then seek a school that works with special-needs kids. Volunteer and offer respite work. Ideally this would be an ongoing thing. Getting involved with Special Olympics is great, too. Your girls will be more impacted than the kids they help."

—AMY JACOBER, AZUSA PACIFIC UNIVERSITY

A group I know has scheduled a summer trip to visit a secular nonprofit organization in Florida that grants children with terminal diseases, ages 3 to 18, their dying wishes. The church will take students to serve these children in tangible ways. They'll paint, do maintenance work around the property, and plan and host a Christmas party, since these children may not make it to December.

In our selfish culture, it's important that we learn how to recognize and meet others' needs. The more opportunities you give your girls to live lives of service, the more they will find their lives as they give themselves away.

The Women's Ministry at Your Church

The women of your congregation may be involved with something where they need more hands. As the girls join with them in serving others, they'll build relationships with these older women and see the value of lifelong service. Your girls could even help with your church's Vacation Bible School. Julie and her girls offered to completely clean up after a women's minis-

try event. When they finished, they went to do something fun together. Tagging service with a bonding experience is a great way to foster a lifestyle of serving others.

Sharing Their Faith

I was always challenging my girls to share their faith, but then I realized that I rarely gave them practical advice on how to do it. So many of your girls probably want to witness to their friends, but they may need encouragement and tips for how to share their faith. Offer training for your girls in how to write their testimonies and then share them with a seeker. Help them memorize key Scriptures and the core elements of the gospel. Have them practice sharing their faith with each other so they feel more comfortable when they're in a real-life witnessing situation. One girls' minister I know tells about how during training, one of her girls realized that she wasn't a Christian and that she needed Christ. She prayed to receive him right there in the training session.

Give your girls real-life opportunities to witness. Encourage them to pray for the people they will witness to, and then take them out to share their faith. Prayer is key—for themselves and for the people who will hear the gospel. You may want to go to a mall or another location where you know there will be lots of people. Make sure your girls know that while witnessing is important on a mission trip, our biggest mission opportunity is in our daily lives. Give your girls the idea of making a list of non-Christians for whom they can pray daily. The more they pray for their non-Christian friends, the more they'll see God's hand working in those friends' lives.

Make sure you emphasize the relational part of witnessing. The more they offer friendship to others, the more chances they'll have to talk about their faith. Teach your girls to be influencers in the circles where God has placed them. If they're on the soccer team, that's their primary mission field. Likewise, if they sing in the school choir, these are the people whom God has placed in their lives to hear about him. The more girls can see the platforms God has given to them as ways to serve others, the more they will make a real and lasting impact. Encourage them to be a part of God's work in the lives of the people they know and to join in fulfilling his purpose for their generation.

When girls see you model a lifestyle of witnessing, they'll be more likely to have the boldness to follow your example. Let your girls know that it's okay to be scared to witness or to not know how to start a spiritual conversation. Make sure they understand that when they're authentic before their friends and when they truly care about them, God will give them opportunities to speak truth in love.

Helping Our Girls Become Mission-Minded

It's easy for us to become so focused on the details of the ministry we're involved with that we forget about the world beyond the borders of our own country. The fact is, the more opportunities we give girls to think about and actually participate in mis-

"It is so important to help girls develop God's heart for the nations."

—JANÉE ANGEL

sions as young adults, the more apt they will be to live with a broader vision of the world.

If your church has a significant missions focus, your job will be simpler. You can easily plug your students into many of the opportunities your church offers. However, if your church lacks this focus, you will have to work that much harder to help your students shift their gaze outward. But don't get discouraged; there is so much you can do to expose your students to missions—across the hall at school and around the globe.

Do you give your students opportunities to step outside their comfort zones? Do you train them in how to relate to people who aren't like them with the hopes of eventually sharing the gospel with them? Ask someone you know who is skilled in this area to teach your girls. Are there missionaries from your church who are home on furlough for the summer? If so, make sure your girls get to know them. As much as you can, give these missionaries a platform with your girls. Ask them to share about their work, the people they minister to, and their needs. If girls personally know some missionaries, they will be able to put a face on the concept of missions.

Needs in Your Community

Are there places you can serve in your community that will give girls a taste of missions? You may want to plan a one-day mission trip or even ask girls to make a yearlong commitment to a particular area of town where you want to minister. Learn your city. Find out the demographics, income, and level of education, and then share that information with your girls. The more they realize that not everyone in their city looks and acts like them, the more their focus will shift beyond themselves. You may have a significant number of immigrants who live in your community. Find out what their needs are and take a team of your girls to help them. Maybe some residents need conversational English skills. Or you could offer a Bible club for children in an area where a lot of internationals live. The more you expose your girls to the beautiful tapestry of people that God has made, the more likely they will be to get out there and really help them.

Sponsoring Children

Together as a girls' ministry, you may want to sponsor a child in another country and monthly send a check to help support her needs, as well as write her letters and send pictures of the group. Or you might decide on a region of the world or an unreached people group that your girls will collectively pray for. Your girls could learn about the culture, religion, challenges, and needs of this people. Encourage them to follow the news that relates to this group of nationals. Pray for them as a group and challenge your girls to pray for them individually.

Shoe Drives

Have you ever considered holding a "shoe drive" with your girls? There are millions of orphans around the world without even one pair of shoes. Smaller children seem to get more things sent to them, but teenagers are often the forgotten orphans. Many of them live in terrible conditions and need the hope and love of Christ. So many of our girls have closets full of shoes, and if they knew that some girls their age didn't even have one pair to call their own, they would go out in a minute and buy them some.

Why not partner with a ministry that provides shoes for orphans? One such organization is Buckner Orphan Care International in Dallas. They collect and ship new shoes to orphans around the world. They ask for new shoes because of customs regulations and because it's also good for the girls to make a sacrifice, rather than just cleaning out all of their old shoes. You could host a "Shoe Sleepover," where everyone brings a new pair of shoes and socks.

You could also plan an event called "Stuff the Shoes," where a youth group purchases several pairs of teenager-sized shoes, and then girls, friends, and neighbors fill the shoes with cash to pay for more shoes or for shipping costs. Sometimes it's fun to hold a contest between different groups to see who can stuff the most shoes. You could also try this idea with girls versus boys, where girls stuff cash inside girls' shoes and boys put their money inside boys' shoes.

Another good idea is a "Shoe Shower," where girls gather at someone's house to play games involving shoes and then watch a movie such as Cinderella, which has an orphan theme and in which a pair of shoes plays a big role. They serve food with "soul" and then collect the shoes that all the girls brought to donate to the orphans. To help with preparation, Buckner will send promotional materials and a step-by-step guide to any organization, school, or church planning a shoe drive. They even host groups that want to work in the warehouse in Dallas, sorting and boxing up shoes for orphans. It's a great way for girls to take a mission trip of sorts, where they reach across the world without leaving the country. A lot of the girls who give shoes take pictures of themselves or write notes to the orphans on the cards Buckner provides, and then stuff these into the shoes. So many of the orphans who receive the shoes sleep with the notes or pictures under their pillows. As girls take part in projects like these, they get opportunities to give sacrificially to those who have a lot less than they do. If you're interested in partnering with Buckner's vision to deliver shoes to orphan souls, check out www.shoesfororphansouls.org.

"Do some research on sweatshops with your girls' help. There are tons of Web sites to get you started. Next take a trip to the mall and talk about being a wise consumer and discuss pragmatic things you can do to make a difference. Your girls will start to understand that their lifestyle choices affect those around the world."

—AMY JACOBER, AZUSA PACIFIC UNIVERSITY

A Mission Trip

While hearing about missions is a wonderful tool to open students to the heart God has for others, greater change takes place when they actually go. Make sure you give your girls the opportunity to participate in a mission trip at some point. If you can't physically plan it, check out one of the great ministries that specialize in leading teams around the country and the world. Various groups take students to help drill wells, hand out food, do prayer walks, and meet practical needs.

"Find stories of organizations and historical movements that began with prayer walks. You may want to include your girls in the process of research. Then give your girls the opportunity to actually participate in a prayer walk."

—AMY JACOBER, AZUSA PACIFIC UNIVERSITY

Or you may want to team up with missionaries affiliated with your church. Your group could help them with handing out tracts and fliers, prayer walking, or simply loving the children of their area. Not only will going across borders change your girls' perspectives, it may alter their ultimate life paths. So many missionaries say that their early exposure to missions formed them and shaped the call of God on their lives to go to the nations.

You may want to take your girls to another city, where you partner with a local church, organization, or ministry. Your girls can support the work already going on in that area and may even be challenged to minister the same way in their own town. A friend of mine took her girls to a major metropolitan area where she exposed them to the very poor while working in soup kitchens and delivering food to AIDS victims. Her girls then helped with an outreach for a church plant by giving out granola bars in a very exclusive area where the upper class lived and worked.

Seek to keep missions in front of your girls. Be certain that even students who don't get to go on a mission trip have the opportunity to learn about missions. Remind them that they are citizens of a larger world that God loves just as much as he loves them. Give them the chance to sacrificially give toward a missions cause. If you hear of a need, present it to your girls. Maybe some missionaries your church is affiliated with need shipments of things or a certain amount of money for their ministries. Present this opportunity to your girls and let them be a part of the answers to prayer.

I heard about a group that held a church-wide yard sale to raise money for the mission trip they were planning. The girls' minister emphasized with her girls that since we are a nation obsessed with stuff, it's good to take steps to de-clutter our lives. Every dollar they made went to the girls' mission trip. Girls took crucial roles in the planning, praying, and raising money that led up to the day they left. When they boarded the plane to go, they were already very focused on the purpose of their trip because they had been working toward getting things ready for so long.

You may want to host an international night where you ask each girl to bring a special dish from another country. Divide the girls into groups, and then have each one share a little bit about the country she chose. You could encourage them to bring any information they have about this nation, such as pictures or souvenirs. At the end of the night, pray in groups for the people in the different countries represented.

You could also invite girls into your home and make or buy the cuisine from a particular country. Show them some in-depth things about the culture and people. You might watch a movie about that country or provide them with some pictures of the work missionaries are doing there. With information so readily available, it's fairly easy to teach about a country with a minimal amount of research. You might even spotlight a missionary who lives there and pray especially for her. Your girls could then write her notes or put together a care package to send to her.

My friend Janée has planned a "Hunger Dinner" with her girls. Girls come to a dinner where she has prepared three different types of meals. One meal is overflowing with food, representing the one-third of the world that's well fed and overfed. Another meal is small, representing the one-third of the world that's malnourished. The last type of meal is just an empty plate, to show the one-third of the world that's starving. When girls arrive, they walk through a line and randomly receive one of the three types of meals. Janée said it was interesting to watch the girls interact with one another and see which girls offered to share with the others. After the meal was over, she talked about the reality of the world hunger problem and what God says about our responsibility as those who have been given so much. She then discussed how they could respond, both personally and as a group, to make a difference.

Take every chance you get to teach your girls about the responsibility they have in the world. Let current events prompt you to pray with your group for believers on the other side of the globe. Teach your girls about unreached people groups, closed countries, and the mission efforts underway around the world. There are countless great teaching tools out there to help you open your students' eyes to missions. You may want to have your girls study the history of different mission movements and learn about what God is doing right now in Iraq or Mexico. Whenever possible, put a face on the word *missions*. Bring in missionaries to talk with your girls and build relationships with them. Share about your own mission experiences and ask your pastor and other church members to share about theirs.

Our girls long to give themselves away to something that's bigger than they are. Ask God to help you present them with opportunities to live out the callings on their lives. Don't underestimate your girls because they're young. God wants to place his hand on these girls and set them apart for his purposes in the world. Keep this big picture in your mind at all times, when talking with your girls, laughing with them, serving together, or when you're by yourself praying for them.

Remember: You Are Not Alone

God is raising up women—young and old—across the globe to minister to this generation of teenage girls. Again, one of the fastest growing staff positions in churches is that of a girls' minister. I pray that this book has provided some practical ideas for you to try with your girls. Let these ideas be starting places. God may lead you to undertake something that has never been tried before. If so, find others to help and support you; then step out and see what he does. Meet those who share your passion and partner with them. Link your arms, efforts, and prayers, and set your gaze to follow him.

A friend of mine constantly says that she doesn't want to be possessive of the resources, ideas, and gifts God has given to her. Her greatest pleasure is in passing them on to others who also want to reach girls. What about you? Are you equipping others by the legacy you're leaving behind? It's never too early—or too late—to begin.